HOLLYWOOD HUCKSTER

A Memoir of Hysterical Proportions

DAVID GARBER

WARNING:

If you are offended by sex, profanity, drugs, nudity, politically incorrect banter, mischievous scandals, shameless antics, questionable schemes and the nasty truth about Hollywood, please stop and close this book. Do NOT read on. If you do so, it is at your own risk.

HOLLYWOOD HUCKSTER

LINZACK PUBLICATIONS

HOLLYWOOD HUCKSTER

A Memoir of Hysterical Proportions

Author: David Garber

Copy Editor: Lori Bjork http://loribjork.tumblr.com/loris411

Cover Design: Lindsay Garber, Lindsay Garber Graphic Designs http://lindsaygarber.com

Published in the United States by Linzack Publications,

ISBN number: 978-1490302171

First Edition: June, 2013

Web address for updates: www.HollywoodHuckster.wordpress.com.

HOLLYWOOD HUCKSTER

FROM THOSE IN THE KNOW

"It's *Mad Men* of the '70s and '80s, set in Hollywood! I loved it!"

Lance Robbins, former President, Fox Family Films

＊＊＊＊＊

"When taking a pitch from Kevin, the buyer always risked getting hit by a beanball. Reading this book, you'll see why."

Jake Tauber, former Vice-president, NBC Network

＊＊＊＊＊

"You only live once, but if you do it right, once is enough – unless you're Kevin Hartigan. *HOLLYWOOD HUCKSTER* is just as I remember him."

Mark McClafferty, former Vice-president, ABC Network

＊＊＊＊＊

"Kevin possessed the skills to walk between raindrops without getting wet – at least until he got drenched. Garber, in this book, explains it all!"

Eric Epstein, Kevin Hartigan's attorney

＊＊＊＊＊

"I knew Kevin and could best describe him in three words, "bona fide nut." Garber captures him perfectly, down to the post-beer burp."

David Winn, actor, The Young and the Restless

HOLLYWOOD HUCKSTER

ABOUT THE AUTHOR

DAVID GARBER

David Garber is an award-winning film and television writer and producer in Los Angeles. He's efforts have resulted in his winning the Television Critics Association Award and the prestigious PRISM Award. His professional career spans 30 years and, as of this publishing, is still flourishing.

In television he's been under contract to CBS, NBC, ABC, Viacom, Eddie Murphy, Glen Larson, Bill Cosby, Aaron Spelling and Redd Foxx. He's served as a writer and/or producer on series as diverse as *The Tonight Show* starring Johnny Carson, *Saved by the Bell*, *The Love Boat*, *Welcome Back Kotter*, *The Bill Cosby Show*, *Power Rangers*, *227*, *The Fall Guy*, and *Alien Nation*.

In features, he's written and produced films for Paramount, MGM, United Artists, 20th Century Fox and Warner Brothers.

HOLLYWOOD HUCKSTER

DEDICATION

To Hava, Lindsay, Zack, Helen, and Kevin – It's been an amazing and indelible journey. Without you, there would be no story—nor for that matter, could there ever have been a me.

HOLLYWOOD HUCKSTER
A Memoir of Hysterical Proportions

TABLE OF CONTENTS

A Memoir of Hysterical Proportions

PREFACE

"When you're in jail, a good friend will be trying to bail you out. A best friend will be in the cell next to you saying, 'Damn, that was fun.'" So said Groucho Marx. So lived Kevin Hartigan.

Who?

Easily the most famous man in Hollywood that you've never heard of.

He achieved the success people only dream about, then lost it.

He attained the power people crave, then misused it.

And he had the money people fantasize about, then squandered it.

His is the quintessential Tinsel Town cautionary tale. And it's all true.

Success in Hollywood is a game – somewhat of a crap shoot. Some people become "players" while others become inconsequential. Those who are good at it prosper. Those who are good at it and talented become Spielberg or James Cameron. Kevin played the game, was among the best at it and reaped its deserved rewards...money. But with his brash behavior, came notoriety. If you did something inexplicably mindboggling or particularly offensive in this entertainment capital, you were said to have pulled "A Hartigan."

From my view at his right side, his partner in crime (and punishment), I witnessed the inner workings. How he got here, what he became, and most assuredly his adventures and misdeeds, is what this book is all about. There's a razor-thin line separating Hollywood genius from Hollywood insanity. Kevin walked both sides.

Some people cause happiness wherever they go. Others *whenever* they go. He was Mr. Comin' 'n Goin'. By the time he finally left, the whole industry breathed a collective sigh of relief. All but me. I saw him take a naïve boy and turn him into a man— a successful Hollywood writer/producer. Without him I could never have achieved a thriving 30+ year career in this town. I may have been no more than the broom and pooper-scooper sweeper behind the elephants at the circus when I started, but I became one of the event's center ring acts before the circus train pulled out of town. That, I owe to my mentor and gregarious 'pachyderm,' Kevin.

*****

Names have not been changed to protect the innocent as no one, not even Popes John Paul I *or* II could honestly claim they were. After all, this was a decade of sex, drugs and rock 'n roll. Now it's time to tell the truth, ruffle some feathers, and pay the piper.

"KUNTA?"

"She was so tough, even her shit had muscles." That's the way Kevin described her.

Lila Garrett was one of the first women to break the glass ceiling and become a writer/executive producer in television. She didn't get there by being meek or mild. She had a temper and overwhelming disposition that could make the weak men cower. She had just written a number of comedy scripts that garnered so much attention that every network wanted her. And that's where Kevin and I entered the picture.

Kevin talked our way onto the 20th Century Fox lot where Lila had offices. He was armed for a mission. If we could impress her, maybe we could leverage that to get ourselves some work. It was late in 1977 and Kevin had just seen an episode she wrote on *Maude*. He knew we three liberals would get along very well.

Lila's assistant greeted us in her office across from the commissary. Kevin claimed we were agents dropping off scripts. She didn't believe us. To glance at us, looking like Mutt and Jeff, I wouldn't have, either. She refused to take our scripts. Kevin and I had no choice, we left.

Driving down Pico on the way home, Kevin spotted a second-hand store. We went inside where he found a box filled with at least 100 damaged ping pong balls. Some were cracked, some were dented, but the owner was just going to toss them out. Kevin asked if he could have them.

I had no idea what he'd be doing with this collection. Yet, I was sure there was a method to his madness or at least some madness to be considered. Kevin took our two sample scripts, put them in the box with as many of the ping pong balls as it could hold, and handwrote a note:

Dear Lila. Now we hope you have enough balls to read our material. Hartigan and Garber.

He signed the note and added our telephone numbers. We gift wrapped the box and had it delivered to her offices.

That night we got a call.

She loved our creativity and read both of our spec scripts. She wanted to talk to us and told us to prepare a few sitcom pilot ideas to pitch to her. She had three networks begging her to come in with pilot ideas. Kevin was going to make sure we got to write one of them. Prior to the meeting, Kevin purchased a large arrangement of flowers and had it delivered to her office. Strung across it was a banner that read:

To Lila Garish – 1st Lady of Pilots *

Next to the asterisk read:

*according to TWA, American, Pan Am and United.

She got the humor. She got us. We were her guys. All we needed now was an idea. And Lila, the ultra-liberal, couldn't pass up the one we pitched: "Under One Roof" – the story of two families sharing a house— one Southern white, the other urban Black.

As Kevin had anticipated, she jumped at it like a desperate virgin on a two-bit whore. She wanted to know the characters.

"The southern white father would be so stupid you'd have to water him. All that separated his wife from trailer trash was she didn't have a ride back to the trailer park! And their kids watched Roots backwards, so it would have a happy ending."

Lila almost choked. "And what about the Black family?"

Kevin smiled, "Think of this show as the difference between a white and a Black fairy tale. The white one begins, once upon a time… and the Black one begins, y'all motherfuckers ain't gonna believe dis shit dat just went down!"

Lila chuckled with a little guilt and asked if Kevin wasn't being a bit racist.

He responded, "Racism is when a white guy runs over a Black guy with his truck. And reverse-racism would be if I backed up. I don't think I'm either."

I jumped in, infectious as the moment was. "The way I see it, the white dad would call 5th grade his senior year. And his school fight song would be, 'Dueling Banjos.'"

It took Lila a nanosecond to see who she was dealing with.

Any questions of whether we could think on our feet disappeared like chocolate at a Weight Watchers buffet. She set up a meeting for us at NBC right then and there.

We escorted Lila to the network offices in beautiful downtown Burbank and were seen immediately by their Veep of Comedy Development, Dick Ebersol. With him was a young associate, Brandon Tartikoff. Just as Lila was the hot female commodity in the industry at that time, Brandon was making a name for himself as the new up and comer with the network honchos. He had supervised a few shows at NBC the previous season which all became hits. He seemed to have the Midas touch. Kevin knew that and played our pitch much more to him than his boss. Then, abruptly, Brandon was called out of the meeting.

Kevin insisted that we hold off until Brandon got back. And vamping was nothing challenging to him. He kept things alive until Brandon returned. When the executive came back, he had some news.

Kevin looked at him and said, "It must be great news because you look like a short-legged fat boy running through a field full of Snickers."

Brandon had been promoted to Sr. Veep of Comedy development. Everyone was stunned except Kevin.

"I hope you took the money and not just the title," Kevin chided.

Awkward as it was, Ebersol could merely be cordial as the shock set in. He had just been leap-frogged by Tartikoff.

Kevin congratulated Brandon on his promotion and said, "Let's not let good news get in the way of a great show."

We continued our pitch. Lila offered a few times that if it would be more appropriate, we could come back another day. Kevin wouldn't hear of it.

"What? And deprive Brandon here of his first purchase in his new position?"

After the pitch, we went to Lila's office back at Fox. There she got a call. The first lady of pilots had another notch in her belt. It wasn't the NBC pilot though. CBS had just purchased a new sitcom series from her. Lila wanted to tell the world about it so we were summarily dismissed until she heard back from NBC about our pilot. She had important calls to make.

Kevin wanted in on that new series with a staff position. We had inside information about the sale. We needed to find a way into an offer before the rest of the industry found out. And he had a plan. After all, Kevin never walked through the front door if you had left the window unlocked for him to crawl through.

The next morning he rang up Lila. When the receptionist answered, he said he was Kunta Kinte, the hero of the recent and landmark epic mini-series, "Roots."

Immediately Lila picked up…"Kunta?"

She really believed all the bullshit Kevin, pretending he was Kunta Kinte, fed her from his end about being so proud of her liberal beliefs, helping free his people from slavery and opening minds with her writings. He wanted to meet her face to face. She was so swept up that she didn't realize the real Kunta Kinte had been dead for over 150 years. She had, like most of America, seen Alex Hailey's "Roots" recently and didn't put two and two together.

This wouldn't be the only time Kevin would pull the wool over executive's eyes. He was great, persuasive and amazing adroit and capturing someone else's character and personality. He could size you up in a nanosecond.

We two writers dropped by Lila's office that afternoon. Lila was so excited. She was going to have lunch tomorrow with her hero – Kunta Kinte. Kevin smiled. Then he produced a small pocket sized memo/tape recorder. He played back Lila's call to her. She'd been punked by him and was so embarrassed. She demanded that tape from him.

He responded, "No story editor on your new show, Baby, I'm Back could possibly refuse that request."

She knew. Kevin had her. She was thinking about it and weighing the embarrassment factor when her assistant buzzed in. Brandon Tartikoff was on the line. Lila took the call. She suddenly was all smiles, thanked him and said she'd be in touch. As she hung up she put out her hand to Kevin for the tape. Instead he shook it, knowingly.

"That was NBC. I guess we're going to be working together on the pilot," she announced. She snapped her fingers, demandingly and opened the palm of her hand for Kevin to drop the tape into it. He hesitated. "Okay. You win. You're both my story editors on *Baby, I'm Back*," she reluctantly confided. "Now give me that tape and get the fuck out!"

Kevin was cooler than an igloo toilet seat on New Year's Eve as he handed her the tape. He ignored her outstretched hand and gave her a truly affectionate hug. She knew from then on what she was dealing with. She'd occasionally refer to us as "Unpredictable & Son."

Soon after that, we became great friends and close allies. But any time Kevin needed to win a creative argument, he'd just look at her and do his Lila impression: "Kunta?"

*****

And here I am, 30 years later and I still have five of these cracked, dented and totally useless ping pong balls from the Lila scam. I can see that cleaning out my home office today wasn't going to be all that easy. I think I'll put these in the "keeper" pile. I still have a lot of stuff to go if I'm ever going to clear enough space to get back to work.

IN THE SLAMMER

Every once in a while, I like to look at the things I've accumulated over the years. They sure bring back memories. Oh, man, here's my Groucho Pez dispenser! I got that back in the '70s. I was wondering where I put that. Do I dare eat one of these little sugary treats left over inside? Okay, I'll try one. I mean don't these things have a shelf life of like a kazillion years? What the hell?

Though I consider myself quite organized, I am a bit sentimental. Over the years I had accumulated all sorts of odds and ends, knick-knacks and bric-a-brac. To me, these items in my home office are my treasures, my memory touchstones. I have my reasons for saving each of them.

Take this Hollywood Map to Dead Star's Graves. How could I throw that out? Short of a zombie uprising, this map would be current forever. Besides, this one came with some personal memories attached— MGM, Aaron Spelling, drugs and a month in a jail cell.

A quick look at my calendar. Could it be 30 years ago already?

*****

It was summer, 1980, when my partner Kevin and I got an interesting ring up from our agent, Herb Karp. It seems Aaron Spelling was getting into the movie business. Building on his television successes like *The Love Boat*, *Charlie's Angels* and *Starsky and Hutch*, he was looking for a toehold in features. For his initial foray into mainstream movies, he had a script written for a film called, *Slammer*. It was to be for prison pictures what the recently released and totally irreverent blockbuster *Airplane!* was to the Airport movie franchise.

Aaron had partnered with MGM on this venture and they were not too pleased with the first draft. So they needed a rewrite. Herb and the others at the William Morris Agency thought Kevin and I would be a perfect fit for this venture. So we were set up for a meeting with Aaron and the MGM vice president of feature development, Billie Trapper. She was one of but a handful of female executives to reach that level in this "all boys" town. Though she was powerful, Aaron's power was mightier. So, it was no surprise that the first meeting was held in his opulent office bungalow at 20th Century Fox Studios, from where he ran his TV empire. Billie, like us, was summoned to the mount.

Kevin looked around the lavish, well-appointed suite that must have cost close to the U.S. national budget to decorate. He took it all in and commented, "What happened, Liberace die and leave you all his furnishings? Where's the piano?"

Aaron didn't miss a beat, "If you play, I'll have one brought in."

Kevin smiled back, "If I play piano, we'll have it declared a miracle and you're one step closer to sainthood. The only 88s these fingers are tinkling belong to a pair of size 44 twin strippers I met up in Frisco. At least they said they were twins. I know the one with a 'schwantz' was."

I thought I better step in as Billie was choking at Kevin's run. I didn't want her or Aaron to get the wrong idea. We were here for this job.

That didn't stop Kevin. "Don't listen to David. He's just hoping you validate for parking. Say, this place is really swell. And large. You live here?

Aaron played along. "No, I live in Beverly Hills."

"With all the shows you've got on the air, I'm surprised you don't own Beverly Hills. Change the name to Aaron's Acres or the Spelling Spread. What you need is a Jewish accountant."

"I've got one of those," Spelling confessed.

"That's the problem. You need a few of them – and a *goy* like me to turn your lights on and off during the Sabbath. I'm cheap. No, wait a minute. That's my partner Garber. The other day he took a dollar bill out of his pocket, and I swear I saw George Washington blinking at the light."

Okay, enough of this frivolity. I unwound Kevin as best I could. We listened to Aaron and Billie explaining what they were looking for. From what they described, we were their guys. And they thought so too.

Billie had seen the 5-minute promo we made for an as yet, unproduced movie. Within minutes, we were hired. I'm sure Kevin's high energy entrance didn't hurt us either. So now we were going to be the new writers on this picture, working for a major motion picture studio – MGM.

Herb had arranged for us to have offices on the Fox lot. We preferred MGM, but Aaron really enjoyed Kevin and wanted to keep him close. We were exiled off into some old building with a bunch of other writers. Immediately Kevin set out to stand us apart. After all, we were now major studio feature writers and everyone around us was TV. There is a class system. Despite our lack of class, more like an abundance of crass, we took some creative steps to set distance ourselves.

The first thing Kevin did was try to create an ambiance. He got some thumb tacks and used them to outline the outside of the office door. Then he took black paint and colored the entire portal. Damn if it didn't look just like a cell door, complete with rivets.

Then for the inside, Kevin had found a gag, plastic urinal. He mounted that to the wall and had a cot and a desk brought in. Everything else went. We did have a window. So, Kevin got some doweling, painted the wooden tubes black and put them in the opening. It looked like we had bars interrupting our view to the outside. Then, our dingy walls were the next to be addressed.

Kevin took black paint and started putting up graffiti – on every wall. He painted sayings like - "Don't Pee here," "Birdman of Alcatraz that way (with an arrow)," "for a good time, hire a hooker. For a lot of time, hire my attorney."

Now if Spelling got wind of what we were up to, there was no telling what repercussions we would have faced. We had, in essence, trashed an office. We really changed the look of the room into a prison cell atmosphere. Anytime someone came in to visit us, from "invited" guests to mail room delivery persons, Kevin gave them paint and asked them to write something on the wall. Before long, word got out about our "being in the joint". People— total strangers— came from all over the studio to check it out and paint something on our cell walls. Even the stars of the shows on the lot dropped by to put up something clever – Robert Wagner, all three of *Charlie's Angels*, Lee Majors, even Alan Alda from *MASH*. We had become minor celebs just by decorating.

It didn't take long for Aaron to get word of this. Soon Spelling, the almighty, deigned us with a visit to see for himself what we had done. He knocked on our cell door, catching Kevin rolling a joint which didn't seem to faze him a bit. As Kevin put it, "A joint for the joint. Makes the time go by faster."

With our boss's entrance, Kevin got out the paint and a brush and told Spelling that he needed to put his mark on the wall. Interestingly, at this time, Aaron was going through a lawsuit on *Charlie's Angels* with the creators, Ivan Goff and Ben Roberts. This brouhaha had grown so big that it was all over the papers and the news. Due to the huge star power attached, it was the talk of the town, if not the nation. Even the District Attorney for Los Angeles became embroiled in this coverage.

Things weren't looking too good in this criminal suit for misreported profits – at least if you were Spelling. So, very good-naturedly, the big executive decided to get into the act. He took the paint from Kevin, found a prime spot that had yet to have any graffiti on it, and proceeded to add his touch. The ever dignified and proper Mr. Spelling stroked out on the wall, in large letters, "F. U. DA." Wow! Kevin vowed that when we were finally done with the movie, he'd cut out that piece of wall and save it— for posterity or blackmail— you couldn't be sure.

Before long, perhaps only a month, the script for *Slammer* was completed. It was as wild and crazy as we could make it. It out

Airplaned, *Airplane!*. Aaron read the script and thought it was wonderful, crazy and outrageous. That was our goal. So, on the heels of his great reaction, Kevin asked if we could have the pleasure to deliver the script to Billie Trapper over at MGM. Aaron could see no harm in it, so he agreed. Oh, how naïve.

Granting us permission would haunt Aaron for years to come.

Kevin went to work planning our script delivery. I didn't know exactly what he had in mind, but he wanted to make certain this event would be memorable. And with a request like that, you just knew he had something outrageous planned.

He called Billie to tell her the script was ready. We wanted to get it in her hands right away – but we wished to deliver it ourselves. She said she couldn't wait and would clear away all of her appointments for tomorrow from noon on. Kevin said we'd take her to lunch.

The next day we swung by Billie's MGM office building and picked her up in a huge, stretch limo. Kevin had already given the driver the directions to our first stop. As we drove off the lot, Kevin popped open a bottle of expensive champagne and poured for all three of us. We lifted our crystal glasses with a toast and began the day's journey. When Billie inquired where we were going to eat, Kevin said, "We're going to a quiet place to enjoy a picnic meal. Oh, and we're having a surprise celebrity join us."

During the ride we played 20 Questions, trying to figure out who this celebrity might be. Billie and I narrowed it down to singer/actor/male/movies. Did Kevin arrange for Sinatra? Fred Astaire? Elvis?

"Bigger." That's all we could get from Kevin.

During our guessing game Kevin picked up the car phone, though I hadn't heard it ring. We could only listen to his side of the conversation. "Sounds perfect. Put me down for 1,000 shares," then he hung up the limo phone.

"Sorry. That was my broker with a tip. Seems that Fairchild Electronics just announced they're merging with Honeywell Computers. How can you go wrong with the new company called Fairwell Honeychild?

Billie and I looked at each other and chuckled.

Kevin continued on. "Go ahead and laugh — but I made a killing when Golden West merged with Dainty Showers. Who'd have thought there'd be that much money in Golden-Showers?" His humor was refreshing, even if the images he conjured weren't. But restraint was never Kevin's long suit.

Within a few minutes we pulled into Hillside Cemetery in Culver City, just minutes away from the studio. We got out and Kevin asked the driver to bring the picnic basket over to this large gazebo, Al Jolson's monument. There, next to the statue of Jolson on his knee we set our spread. Inside the giant, six columns, stone structure was the crypt holding the old star's remains. Billie commented that when Kevin said we'd be having a fourth join us, a celebrity, she assumed a living one.

Kevin said, "You know what a ham 'Joley' was? He's even going to sing for his supper." He then pushed a button on the side of the crypt and damn, if from the overhead speakers, it didn't rain down upon us the voice of Jolson, himself, belting out, "Mammy."

Billie and I struggled to contain ourselves. While Jolson sang "Where the sun shines best..." Kevin prepared a sandwich and placed it on the alabaster crypt. He spoke to the monument, "They were out of pumpernickel. I got you rye."

But our afternoon was just beginning. After we ate, we climbed back in the limo and directed the driver – "Hollywood Park," the local horseracing track. While Kevin rolled a joint, which the three of us enjoyed, he handed Billie a $50 dollar bill and asked for her favorite number from one to 12. She chose six.

We arrived at the track and all marched up to the better's window. Kevin told Billie to put the 50 bucks on horse six, for the next race. We then went to the field which Kevin had prearranged for us to enter and were shown to our private box. We watched the next race, rubbing elbows with the rich and famous. When it was over, Billie had won $400. Kevin remarked how much more she could have won if her horse hadn't been the favorite. She cashed in her winning ticket and we were on the move again. Kevin gave our private box tickets to some old reprobate who was rummaging through the garbage. We got back into the limo and drove off. It wasn't the idea of giving the unfortunate derelict the prime seats that made Kevin smile. No, what did that was thinking about the faces of the well-heeled, upper class folks seeing this bum enter their inner sanctum. He'd have loved being a fly on the wall for that entrance, but we had places to go.

Another joint and lots of champagne later, we were at our next stop: the bowling alley where Kevin and I waited out getting our first job, a few short years back. Since that time, we considered the bowling alley to be our good luck joint. We put on our shoes while Kevin went and got a tray full of drinks— peppermint schnapps— for our "shot" frames. Before we could bowl the odd number frames, we had to down a shot.

Now I have to say Billie was quite the trooper. She could really hold her liquor. She also spoke just like a sailor with a few drinks in her. Damn, what a woman! And now the queen was plunging her fingers into a bowling ball.

The kegling was filled with booze and lots of backstage tattletales. While waiting for the pin reset machine which jammed, Kevin and Billie started talking about life in general. Then it segued somehow to religion, not always a safe subject. By then we were tipsy and most of the rules went out the window.

Kevin asked if Billie went to confession.

"Occasionally. Why?" she replied.

"It's just you talking about your husband's teenage years and it got me thinking about mine… My mother used to make me and my younger brother, Eugene, go to church every Sunday. I even had to become an altar boy.

Billie snickered, "That must have been something."

"The last time I went, I confessed to having sinned. I'd been with a loose girl. Father Flaherty then asked me, '…And what girl would that be?'"

Kevin downed another jigger of schnapps. Continuing, he shared that he refused to give up her name because he didn't want to ruin her reputation. "'Was it Mary Elizabeth Colleary?' I hesitated. 'I cannot say, Father.' 'Was it Teresa O'Leary?' I just shook my head. Father Flaherty continued, 'Anna Laney?' I didn't answer. 'Cathy O'Connor?' My lips were still sealed. 'Was it Rose Marie Toole, then?' Father Flaherty sighed in frustration. I remember his words like they were yesterday. 'You're very tight lipped, Kevin Hartigan, and I admire that.'"

"So what happened?" Billie asked.

"He told me I had to atone. He gave me a bunch of 'Hail Marys' and I had to give up being an altar boy for 4 months."

Billie felt Kevin got away pretty easy.

"When I walked back to my brother, Eugene, he wanted to know what Father Flaherty gave me, too. I proudly confessed, 'Four months of vacation and five good leads.'"

The pin machine was back running. Tipsy as we were, we finished our game. We were about as close to drunk as you could be. Billie felt we should get her back to the studio while she could still stand – or at least give that impression.

So we straggled into the limo and headed for the Metro Goldwyn Mayer lot. Kevin shared with Billie how her studio got its name.

"I don't know if you knew this, but Samuel Goldwyn was actually Samuel Goldfish. He changed his name later on, like many Jews in the entertainment business. At the time he was partnered with Edgar and Archibald Selwyn. Then Louis B. Mayer joined them. So the four men were trying to come up with a name for their studio and considered combining portions of their last names. They decided to call the studio Goldwyn-Mayer which made sense when you think of the option: YerSelfish Studios. True story."

Kevin had two final surprises for Billie. One was the script which she excitedly took from him. She promised to read it right away. The other was a tab of "orange sunshine" or as most people generically call it, a tab of acid. "Something to help you understand what we wrote."

He had one for each of us and said we should all take it, then go up to Billie's office and watch her read the script.

I couldn't believe it. I'd never dropped acid. And I didn't know Kevin to do so either. How could he possibly invite the vice president of this major studio to trip out? Kevin went first. Billie, believe it or not, took the tab, put it on her tongue and washed it down with a shot of tequila from the limo bar. They both looked at me. What choice did I have?

"Fucked up, here I come."

And so the limo dropped us off. We escorted Billie inside. By the time we arrived in her office, things were starting to happen. We sat there as she opened the script. Words started pouring out. No, literally, in my hallucinogenic state, words were actually lifting off the page and floating. I think I even tried to catch them to place them back on the page, but they were too fast for me.

Sometime later, hours for sure, our limo driver came up and found the three of us sitting, just staring blankly into space. He corralled us, safely depositing each of us at our respective homes. Kevin had given him the addresses in advance, just in case.

We had taken the trip of a lifetime, in more ways than one. We dined with a dead celebrity, won a bet on the horses, bowled ourselves drunk, then dropped acid, and finally chased words through space. Now that's what Kevin called delivering a script.

*****

For whatever reason, I was left the map to dead stars graves when the driver dropped me off. Now I couldn't let go of it. It just had too much meaning. So I'm putting that in the ever-growing "save" pile. I was realizing that tossing things out was not going to be that easy a job.

CHUTZPAH

"Yes, I'm tossing stuff out!" I yelled back to my wife who was checking on the progress of my getting rid of all the junk (her word, not mine) in my office project. In truth, I hadn't done much more than blow away some of the dust that had been collecting on my treasures. I mean I had all kinds of valuables here like a pitted, well-tarnished hood ornament off of Charlie Chaplin's 1938 Pierce Arrow. That was the last year they made that car. And it was Chaplin's. I can't get rid of that or this: a hair brush that once belonged to Lucille Ball. Betcha that would bring in a pretty penny on eBay. Not letting go of that. Or this: a plastic snow globe that says inside, *"Chutzpah."*

What, you might ask, is the meaning of the word, *"chutzpah?"* It's a Yiddish word meaning insolence or audacity. To different people it means different things: nerve, guts. In Kevin Hartigan's world it took on a life of its own — total denial of personal responsibility.

*****

In the late '70s, Kevin could see the writing on the wall that variety programming was on the wane and sitcoms were cropping up faster than erections at a Parisian brothel. So "Operation Sitcom" was launched.

We were going to need a spec sitcom script. We didn't exactly know what the most current styling and formatting should be or even how many pages it should run. Kevin was in a hurry. He called up Herb Karp, our agent, to ask him to send us over a couple of produced scripts from some hit shows.

That afternoon a messenger from the Morris Agency delivered two scripts to us; one was an *Alice* episode and the other was a *Sanford and Son*. We read them both and liked the *Sanford* better. Then Kevin went to the sofa, which meant I was going to the typewriter. He looked over to me and said we should have a script done in a day, two at the most.

"Are you crazy?" I shot over to him.

Kevin calmly responded, "Look, the hard work has been done for us. We'll just take this script, rewrite every joke based on what's here, and we'll have a professional and much improved script in no time. We can write better jokes and we already know that the story works."

Damn, that was an amazing idea and that took "*chutzpah.*"

So we wrote an episode of *Sanford and Son* totally original in words, while quite parallel in story. If you put the two works side by side, they would be totally unalike, yet totally the same. The pacing we knew would be right on. Where they had a joke, we had a joke. Where they had some heart, we had some heart – or treacle as it's called in the trade. Where their story was about someone trying to retrieve a misplaced cremation urn from the junk yard, ours was about Fred Sanford's relocating lost love letters his son accidentally tossed away. And it wouldn't be a true Sanford if it didn't include Fred's immortal staggering around and a skyward bellow, "Hold on, Elizabeth, I'm coming to join you, honey!"

Just as Kevin called it, we were done in a day. We were ready.

The method to getting a writing assignment in the mid-'70s was simple. Once a new show was picked up, the executive producers would hold private screenings for selected groups of writers — those whose work they had read and liked or those they knew and had worked with prior.

As we didn't fit into the latter group, we had to get invited in. But how? We could have our agents submit our work but then it might just sit on someone's desk and not get read. Kevin couldn't let that happen, so he took matters into his own hands.

Thus we began another offensive. One thing Kevin never lacked was an "offensive."

Kevin knew that all we needed was just a way through the door to the screenings. His plan was twofold. First he called up the vice president of comedy development at each network. He asked their assistant who the executive producers were on the new shows, and then would charm them into giving us the exec producer's office phone numbers. That was step one.

Step two was Kevin calling these show-runners and telling their assistants that the network had suggested we call.

Kevin would say, "They even gave us your number. Told us to ring you to schedule a time to come by and see the pilot."

In essence, from that call, you'd draw the conclusion that we were coming with the networks tacit approval, blessing or even at their suggestion. And it never failed.

That took "*chutzpah.*"

If they asked to see our material, we would tell them we'd like to deliver it ourselves to ensure it didn't get lost in the pile of other submissions. That too worked every time. When we'd come in to drop off our *Sanford and Son* script, Kevin would get the assistant to see if we could pop our heads in to introduce ourselves and say "Hi" to the execs running the show while we were there. He was always sure to remind everyone that the script was coming in because of the network's suggestion.

The first show we maneuvered our way into was a brand new sitcom called *Carter Country*. The assistant to the executive producers was named Pam Varney. In retrospect, we could credit her with our becoming bona fide sitcom writers... indirectly, anyway.

She bought all of the blarney that came from Kevin. Based on the implied network recommendation, she had us come right over and bring our spec script in. She'd see to it that her bosses, Doug Arango and Phil Duran, would read it that night. Kevin's philosophy: have the assistant on your side and you could get the boss to do damn near anything.

By the time we finished talking to her while dropping off the script, she had arranged for us to come in the following day, to see the next pilot screening.

The offices were on the Golden West Studios lot, on Sunset Boulevard in the heart of Hollywood. In the 1920s, this facility was the home of the Warner Brothers Hollywood Studios. It was on that very site that *The Jazz Singer*, credited with being the first talkie, starring Al Jolson, was filmed. In the ensuing years it was bought by Paramount Pictures. Later it was renamed the Golden West Studios when cowboy Gene Autry bought it. The names had changed, but the facility had not. It was old and creaky – even spooky at night.

We made our way to the production offices to screen the pilot and were shown into the sizable writer's room, set up with a TV monitor and about ten chairs. On the counter was an old coffee maker so ancient that when it was new, coffee hadn't yet been invented.

Slowly a few other writers entered and took seats around us. Then Arango and Duran entered with their secretary, Pam. The two execs seemed to know everyone there but us. They introduced themselves. Pam quickly and efficiently reminded her bosses that it was the vice president of comedy at ABC who had recommended us. That was certainly good enough for Phil and Doug.

Just before starting the tape, Doug said that after we all viewed the show we should go home, think up some story ideas, work them out, and then call to schedule a pitch meeting through Pam. Then they left us to watch the pilot. As soon as the tape finished, Kevin yanked me out of the room. Within moments we were facing Pam at her desk.

"We lied," Kevin started out. "Actually, we saw the pilot over at the network and we ALREADY had ideas. When's the first open appointment for Doug and Phil?"

On the way home, I asked Kevin what that was all about. "There are only so many good ideas," Kevin spewed. "We don't want to give anyone else a chance to get in there before us."

That was "*chutzpah.*"

When I reminded him we'd need ideas, he assured me we'd have them.

We'd need them fast because Pam had set us up to pitch to the two executive producers early the next morning.

The rest of that afternoon we spent tossing around all kinds of ideas. We fleshed five of them out as best we could. Then Kevin cautioned, "If we're lucky enough that they bite on one of our stories, let's not pitch the others."

"We don't want to compete with ourselves. If you give them two good ideas, they'll have to choose between them. We're better off coming back and selling them the second one later."

This made sense to me. Of course, saying and doing are often two different things, especially with this guy.

The next day we were sitting face to face with the creators and executive producers of the show who we had just met the day before. Pam, their secretary, was in to take notes. Just prior to us beginning our pitch, Phil and Doug mentioned they had read our Sanford script the night before and were very impressed.

"We see why the network sent you guys over. You really got the show down perfectly."

"I'm sure we can do the same for you on yours," Kevin replied with the slightest of impish smiles.

Perhaps that was a bit of *"chutzpah"* as well.

Before we could start, two well-dressed men showed up who Arango and Duran seemed quite deferential to. They stood and introduced us to Saul and Bernie. We recognized them by those first names – they were Turtletaub and Orenstein— among the biggest sitcom executive producers in all of TV. And included in their show-running credits was – *Sanford and Son*. Oh, God. What did we get ourselves into?

To make matters a bit more interesting, Phil and Doug said that Saul and Bernie were going to sit in on the pitch meeting. It seems they too were executive producers on this series. They were overseeing a few shows while Arango and Duran were strictly running *Carter Country*. As the introductions concluded, Doug mentioned that he and Phil had just read our sample script and loved it.

"They wrote a spec *Sanford*," Doug shared, referring to Kevin and me. "They nailed your show perfectly."

"You'll have to let us read it," Saul said. "Maybe we could use it!" he smiled.

Little did he know… they already were. So if the pressure wasn't already on, now we had the sword of Damocles hanging right over our heads. Yet that's the kind of pressure Kevin thrived on while I, on the other hand, was shitting bricks.

"Well, let's hear what you've got for us," chimed Bernie.

Kevin started pitching the first of our stories while Pam took copious notes. My partner's pitch started with what we had prepared but grew and grew as he went along. When suggestions or questions were asked by the exec producers, Kevin seamlessly integrated those into our presentation. He was really on top of his game. When he was done, it was evident that everyone was on board.

Pam handed the page of notes she took on that story to Doug. He picked up a thumb tack from his desk and stuck it to the wall. "This one's a keeper."

That sure was music to my ears. Then came the dulcet tones from Turtletaub, "Let's hear the next one."

I shared, "We have other stories. But if you like this one, why don't we concentrate on that?" I was just taking Kevin's advice.

"Forgive my partner," Kevin smiled. "He just didn't want to muddy the waters with our embarrassment of riches."

Kevin proceeded to pitch two more stories. God, he was good. I'd toss in little jokes that we had previously discussed when coming up with these ideas and they went over like gangbusters. Each time we were asked a question, we had the answer, as well as a joke to justify our choice of direction... No one danced as well as us that day. We were Fred Astaire and Gene Kelly gliding seamlessly and effortlessly through an extravagant Busby Berkeley production number.

After each pitch, Pam would hand Doug the notes and he'd stick them to the wall. Three pitches - all home runs.

Now what were we going to do? We knew that at best they would only pick one story, which meant we might lose out on the others. While Kevin was shuffling his notes to pitch the fourth idea, I grabbed his papers and said, "That's all we have at this time." Kevin shot me that innocent, playful furled lip of his. He knew I was doing the right thing. He just needed the bartender to stop serving him.

Doug and Phil looked over to Saul and Bernie. They asked who our agent was and said he'd hear from them in a day or two. As we were leaving, Kevin inquired which story they were leaning toward. They said they'd have to talk it over.

Out in the hallway, as we walked down toward the exit, Kevin stopped and told me he'd meet me at the car. He'd left something back in the offices. So I continued on and waited for him where we parked. I was becoming ever so confident they'd buy one of the stories.

Then it hit me like a bug against a speeding car's windshield – what if Orenstein and Turtletaub decided to read our spec Sanford script? We'd be found out as frauds. Certainly, as executive producers of the show, Turtletaub and Orenstein would recognize it. Our goose would be cooked.

When Kevin got back to the car he noticed I was a bit apprehensive. I shared my fears. While unlocking the car he just smiled and assured me not to worry. When I asked him why, he opened his briefcase and produced the two copies of the *Sanford* script we wrote.

He had returned to the office, convinced Pam that he forgot to bring along copies of our *Sanford* script and said we'd needed them for the next meeting we were going to. She generously retrieved Doug and Phil's copies and gave them to him. One step ahead of me again. That too, was "*chutzpah.*"

The drive home was exciting. We were confident they were going to buy one of our ideas. But which one?

We didn't have to wait long. Our agent Herb had gotten call from Turtletaub. They didn't want any one of the stories we pitched. They wanted all three. They offered us *multiples*, as it's referred to in the trade. How good was that?

Evidently not good enough – at least for Kevin. He said, "If they liked us that much, thought our stories that good, then they'd have to give us a deal to do four **AND** throw in an office on the lot for good measure."

Herb didn't want to go back with that demand. It would make us look ungrateful for their offer. Here we had never written a sitcom script together before. How could we turn down three?

Kevin, as he was want to do, would remind Herb that *WE* were the clients and *HE* was to do what *WE* asked. So he did.

Ten minutes later Herb called back and said the answer was, "No. The original offer stood and that was it. Take it or leave it."

I told Kevin, "We should take this and be thrilled. We went there to sell one. Now we had three."

"Four and an office or no deal." That was Kevin's marching orders back to Herb. "And make it happen."

The next morning just before noon, Herb stopped by my house. Kevin and I were plotting out what our next step would be. Herb said he wanted us to come with him to lunch. I was sure he was going to take us out to try to talk some sense into Kevin and to accept the *Carter Country* offer. But that wasn't the case.

He stopped at Kentucky Fried Chicken and ordered up a bucket at the drive through. Kevin and I were both thinking the same thing, "some lunch with all the money the William Morris Agency was making."

We continued to drive for about five minutes then found ourselves at the gate of the Golden West Studios lot. Herb looked over to the guard, "I'm just here to drop off Hartigan and Garber at their new offices."

Turtletaub and Orenstein had caved. We got the four episodes **and** the offices. That too, was *"chutzpah."*

Even with this win, it didn't take long for Kevin to be "Kevin." During the middle of a story meeting the first week we were there, Saul Turtletaub stuck his head in our office to see how we were doing. We told him of a gag we were working on. Turtletaub said he didn't like it. He thought it was wrong for this particular character.

Saul explained, "The character of Harley is naïve, not stupid."

Kevin bristled and became defensive and attacked one of the gags Saul had put in a recent rewrite he and his partner had done. That ignited a heated exchange between these two over "naïve" vs. "stupid."

Saul stared down Kevin, "I'll make it easy for you. It's my way or you're fired. Losing this job would be *naïve*."

Kevin wasted no time in response, "Saul, you hired us to do 4 of your first 13 episodes. Firing us now would make you and Bernie laughing stocks of the industry. Now that wouldn't be naïve, *that* would be **stupid**!"

And that's the meaning of "*chutzpah*."

We stayed on for the four episodes, as well as picking up assignments on five other shows, all because we had this gig and an office on the lot. This gave Kevin and me credibility.

*****

Standing in my office, stirring up the snow in the globe I reminisced, sometimes it pays to have "*chutzpah*."

THE CALL

I hadn't made my first trash dumpster run yet. That's probably because I hadn't yet found anything I was willing to part with. If I didn't move any faster, this would be spring cleaning 2014, not 2012. When my cellphone rang it was a great excuse to halt my office cleanup chores, at least temporarily.

The composed and recognizable voice on the other end was filled with the unmistakable Boston accent that was oh so familiar to me, a Massachusetts native son. It was good ol' Helen, or "Dear" as Kevin affectionately referred to his wife. She was blessed with spirit, spunk, and a lot of patience to put up with that man. I know. Business partners work days and nights, weekends and holidays, elbow to elbow. In a way we figuratively become the "other" wife. During our ten years of partnership matrimony, I actually spent more time with him than he did with Helen and his kids.

Helen's call began with a few shared observations of freshly arrived springtime in New England. The snow was gone. Tulips, daffodils and crocuses were now in bloom. The Red Sox would soon be back in Fenway Park and the frigid chill was now absent in the daytime air. All were seasonal welcomings to wash away the bitter winter's gloom.

Unfortunately, the call took a bit more somber tone as it went on. I could sense something ominous, kind of that eerie feeling you get walking into a Halloween haunted house. You knew something was afoot but couldn't put your finger on it. You thought you were prepared, but not really.

"David," she asked. "Are you still on the waiting list for a liver donor?"

Reluctantly, I confided I was placed on the national donors' list – a compilation of needy people about the thickness of the Des Moines phone directory. Kevin was among the few who knew this. I hadn't even shared it with my own family. Face it; you have a better chance of winning the "Big Ball" lottery. I enjoy my domestic tranquility. I wasn't about to upset that with information sure to cause unwanted fret, especially if that something is a situation I couldn't control.

"Kevin just suffered a massive stroke. He wants you to have his liver," she reported as calmly as Brian Williams, Diane Sawyer or even Wolf Blitzer might have delivered the evening news.

I had spoken to him but a few weeks before, on his 67th birthday. He sounded fine. I was dumbstruck.

"It's bad David. We've summoned the family. I even called a priest. His last conscious words to me were 'offer liver to David.'"

The first thing I told Helen was not to let the priest in. Few things irritated Kevin more than religious dogma. I thought, "No one knew better than me how Kevin thinks."

"If he woke up and saw that priest standing over him, Kevin would think he was dead and he'd give up fighting for sure."

The call was cut short by the doctor coming into the hospital room to consult with Helen. She said she would call me back as soon as she knew more, "...but I think he's going fast, David." Click.

Irony set in. I was the non-drinker and it was his liver that was being offered to me. Kevin's liver, as he himself would describe it, "was abused worse than a red-headed stepchild or a lazy rented mule."

I tried going back to sprucing up my office. All I could think about was this call. It just didn't seem real. Even so, there was still a chance he'd recover. Helen did leave that door open. Anything was possible. Kevin taught me that.

Then something caught my eye. It was a bottle of beer that had been sitting on my desk shelf for some 30 plus years, hidden away behind a pile of office debris. Two decades and three house moves later, it must be as flat as Abe Lincoln's EKG.

At that moment, none of it mattered. I found a church key and opened the bottle. Remembering back to the day Kevin gave me the brew, I took the opportunity the first swig afforded and offered up a toast in his honor.

"Hey Mabel. Black Label! Carling Black Label Beer." That was one of the most popular slogans in advertising from the 1950s through the '80s. It was a long journey to, "Hey Mabel. Get off the table! The quarter's for the beer." That was Kevin's take on the jingle and the words staring at me on the gift card attached to the six-pack now in front of me.

My eyes started to well up. As I scanned my office, there were so many things, so many "tchotchkes" that reminded me of that golden era. That time when Kevin was the King of Chutzpah. That time when he marched into MGM president Dick Shepard's office with two enormous, live lions on leashes – to show the executive he really knew how to make Hollywood roar. Despite scaring the shit out of the studio head, Kevin and I, along with the lions, marched out with a two picture deal at Metro.

Where would I be without him around any longer? He had to pull through. Not just for me, but for the ages. And I took another chug.

I held steadfastly to the thought that he was going to make it because Kevin never did anything by the book. As the moments wore on, I was being carried back in time to a place that no longer exists but in my mind. That's what crushing news and a flat beer can do to you.

I cleared off an imaginary place for him to recline on my sofa as if he was there. Soon I heard him recalling one of his favorite stories – the one he loved to tell about his wife Helen meeting up with him on a shoot we were doing outside of Tucson. Helen, on her own, drove all the way out from L.A. soon after she had moved out to the City of Angels from her native Boston. She was travelling through a remote part of Arizona when her car broke down. An American Indian on horseback came along and offered her a ride to a nearby town. Not being much of a horse person, yet needing the lift, she climbed up behind him on the horse and they rode off. The ride was uneventful, except that every few minutes the Indian would let out a "Y-e-e-e-h-a-a-a-a!" so loud that it echoed from the surrounding hills. When they arrived in town, he let her off at the local service station. He yelled one final "Y-e-e-e-h-a-a-a-a!" and rode off, like cowboys do in westerns, into the sunset.

"What did you do to get that Indian so excited?" asked the service station attendant.

"Nothing," Helen said. "I merely sat behind him on the horse, put my arms around his waist and held onto the saddle horn so I wouldn't fall off."

"Lady," the attendant said, "Indians don't use saddles."

If Kevin told that story once, he told it a hundred times. When I used to call him on it being an old joke, he'd remind me, "It's only an old joke if you've heard it before."

I tossed back another quaff of the Carling Black Label beer, followed by an uncontrollable smile, coupled with hope. That week we had lost Ben Gazzara (film great) and Whitney Houston (music great). Though the saying goes, "these things happen in threes," we were not going to lose Kevin Hartigan (television great).

MERRY CHRISTNUKKA

Madcap adventures were not unusual but rather the norm when it came to working with Kevin. I had a little buzz on while returning to my spring cleaning. I discovered, in a pile of my collected odds 'n ends, a Jewish Star Christmas ornament for the top of a celebratory, traditional tree. Another souvenir I couldn't see parting with. To anyone else, it would just be a cheap plastic decoration. For me it's what it represented.

*****

That brisk, windy cold night in '75 I had met my future and his name was Kevin Hartigan.

Every L.A. radio station was saturated with the sounds of José Feliciano singing "Feliz Navidad." It's as if all of Hollywood had suddenly become *un Mondo de los Latinos*. We were white Chicanos sans the zoot suits.

A similar homogenization of two cultures – Jewish and gentile – was evident in the rapidly growing popularity of the Christnukkah party, the "traditional" Christmas tree decorating gathering at a Jewish person's house. This was how young, up-and-coming, 20-somethings of Hollywood celebrated in the mid-1970s. No holiday left behind.

My wife, Hava, and I got to the Richie Goldman's duplex before the arrival of the evening's most anticipated guest. Kevin and Helen would arrive on schedule, just about a half hour late. There was always a fantastical reason for Kevin's tardiness. He wore "misfortune's target" on his back. What would it be this time? Was he held up by The Lone Ranger and Tonto's posse galloping down Wilcox Avenue? Or would it be a meteor hit his car while backing out of his garage? He even tied his tardiness once on being detained because the coroner had to exhume his grandmother's body for a police investigation. No matter. When he arrived, everyone would know it. Not because the front door blew in. Just because it was him.

I recognized Kevin the moment he stepped inside. Rumors and stories preceded his arrival. He was a salt and pepper version of Ernest Hemingway. Nothing so much to look at – moderate height, an unkempt beard, a bit overweight and donned in well-worn casual attire – yet your eyes immediately went to him and his statuesque, red-headed wife, Helen. She looked ten years his junior though they were the same age, around 30.

Suddenly, I was in Kevinland; not to be confused with Neverland. For one thing, in Neverland you never grew up. In Kevinland you aged rapidly and grew beyond your years in a finger snap. Anything and everything was possible save hearing *him* say the word, "never." That was reserved for his bosses cursing after him, "F.U. Hartigan. You'll **never** work in this town, again!"

We partiers assembled, drank, smoked and were entertained by our hostess, Karen Cohen and our host, Richard Goldman, on the piano. Richard is a greatly qualified talent – singer, songwriter, and satirist – sometimes all three at the same time. He made the ultimate host for the event, the Goldman - Cohen Christnukkah party.

It only took Kevin a few moments before the storyteller and raconteur extraordinaire became "herbed up." He blazed a joint, took a seat and started explaining to us that he was late arriving because he had just been to his sister-in-law's house. This was the first time he and Helen had seen Patsy since she had gotten married for the fourth time.

"Patsy wanted her sister Helen's support when she broke some personal news to her new husband. How do I put this?" Kevin treaded, "She was still a virgin."

A bizarre bit of information to share with a group of strangers, my wife and I thought.

"Her husband, Martin, was shocked; stunned was more like it," according to Kevin with slight affectation to his voice. "'Patsy, how can that be? You've been married three times before?'"

"'Well,' she confided, "'my first husband, Eric, was an engineer: he understood the basic process but wanted some time to research, implement, and design a new state-of-the-art method of lovemaking. He wanted me to wait. I'm a good Catholic. I wanted kids. So I got the marriage annulled.'"

We chuckled and with an imposed seriousness of the situation, Kevin went on, though his wife, Helen, was giving him the "stink eye."

"Patsy then shared that her second husband, Gerald, was in marketing: 'although he had a nice *product*, he was never sure how to position it. Those are just some wrinkles, I kept telling him! He never could get it in, so I dumped him, too.'"

We were like fish and Kevin had caught us. He was about to set the hook.

"'My last husband, Tommy, was a stamp collector: all he ever did was... God! I miss him! Death and my yeast infection took him too soon.'"

We roared. Yet Kevin wasn't done. Now he'd reel us in.

"'And so,' my sister-in-law confided as she turned to her new hubby, 'I've married you, Martin. Now, I'm really excited!'"

"Marty, wasn't sure he could live up to her expectations. Noticing this, he remarked, 'Good. But what makes you think I'll be any different from the others?'"

"'Because Martin, you're a lawyer. For sure this time I know I'm gonna get screwed!'"

We had been landed on the deck of the laughing ship, the USS Hartigan.

For the better part of two hours, Kevin held court. His recounting of tales ranged from bar fights in the Merchant Marines to growing up poor in Dorchester, Massachusetts. He held us captive. He lived up to all the hype I had been told, and even more. His thick Boston accent and a little tweak of the Irish glint, instead of hindering actually added to the lilting refrains of his stories. They carried you to far off places, kept you smiling and even belly laughing at his observations.

In the '70s, everyone watched *The Tonight Show* starring Johnny Carson. One of his favorite guests, with over a hundred appearances was the buxom Carol Wayne, AKA the Matinee Lady – or as Kevin would say, the "ditz with the tits."

He deftly segued into recently running into her on his way to an interview at NBC in Burbank. Someone asked Kevin if she looked that "big" in person.

"Let me put it to you this way. If she skipped rope without wearing a bra," he crossed himself before continuing, "she'd lose an eye."

Kevin soon asked the host for another bottle of brewski but Helen told him she thought he had imbibed enough. Most probably he had. Kevin deftly assured his wife he was going to be responsible tonight, as he had been a few nights before.

He turned to the group and proudly boasted, "A couple nights ago, and Helen knows this, I was out for a few pops with some friends. I had one too many beers and then chased it with a margarita. Not a good idea. So sensing I was at least slightly over the limit, I did something I've never done before: I took a taxi home."

We could see that he was using sound judgment.

"Good thing, too. On the way I passed a police sobriety checkpoint. Being in a taxi, they just waved it through. I arrived home safely into my wife's adoring arms, without incident, which, in a way, was a total surprise. I had never driven a taxi before and am not sure where I got it."

He did it to us again.

"And can you imagine my further shock when I woke up the next morning and found out those adoring arms around me weren't

Helen's?" He turned to her, "I love you, Dear." She just slugged him.

So went my introduction to the man who would change my life forever. Now, it wasn't always going to be a pleasant journey, but there were sure to be laughs attached, no matter how bumpy the ride.

CARNAC THE MAGNIFICENT

Only a few days had passed since that Christmas when I unexpectedly received a phone call from the White House operator.

"I'm trying to reach David Garber. Is he available for President Ford?"

I told her I was him and she asked me to hold. There was a brief delay until I heard her say, "Go ahead, Mr. President."

"Holy Shit," I said to myself.

Evidently I uttered it out loud because the man on the other end said, "Pardon?"

Damn, I had just said "shit" to the President. I was off to a great start.

"This is Gerry Ford. I hope I'm not disturbing you or your family on this holiday season?"

Before I could answer, I heard the receiver on the other end drop to the floor followed by a minor disturbance. It sounded like the POTUS fell over something reaching for the phone.

When he got back on he said, "Damn CIA. They keep moving things around the Oval Office. I'm sorry. Look the reason for my call is I want you to do *me*, check that, do *America* a big favor."

When the president of the United States asks for a favor, you've got to at least give it some consideration. "What can I do?"

"I need you to meet with Kevin Hartigan before New Year's. It's a grave matter of national security."

"Cut the shit, Kevin. What do you want?"

Kevin responded, "I gotta get my Gerry Ford down better. I think I sound too much like Chevy Chase."

I was actually somewhat in awe of the elaborate extent Kevin would go just to get me to meet with him. So following up on this wildly creative invite, I drove over to his house. We sat out on the stoop of his DeLongpre Avenue, craftsman style rental in an aging part of Hollywood. I would describe it as seedy and quite rundown— both the neighborhood and Kevin. He had an ever present joint in his mouth as we talked.

"Richie tells me you're a comedy writer."

"Well," I responded, "that might be stretching it. I did sell an episode to *Welcome Back, Kotter* which got me into the WGA. If that makes me a writer, then I guess I am one."

Kevin surprised me when he said he had already read it. He had called the Writers Guild and they gave him a contact for me, my agent, Larry Sugo. Larry was a way-past-his-prime fellow who every time I met with him, found a new way to accidentally dip his tie into his cold and stale cup of coffee. His tie stains were as visible as a cigarette chain smoker's discolorations between his index and middle fingers. Anyway, Kevin got Larry to send over my script claiming to be a producer for some new show. Kevin read it, combined with the good things he heard about me from our mutual friend, Richie, and asked me point blank if I was interested in becoming his writing partner.

I had only just met him. If one tenth of the stories about him were true, he was Peck's bad boy, Dorothy Parker and Groucho Marx rolled into one. And if that's accurate, where do I fit in?

Teaming up with someone like that was something to be considered long and hard. I had to weigh the plusses and minuses. On paper Kevin's minuses seemed to be far outweighing his plusses, at least by reputation.

Variety shows, as opposed to sitcoms and dramas, were flourishing on TV at the time. These shows featured folks like Sonny and Cher, Carol Burnett, The Muppets, Donnie & Marie, Andy Williams and Dean Martin. Basically if you were an entertainer with even the slightest name value, you were given a variety show. Kevin thought that a team like him and me would be a perfect fit to write "these pieces of fluff."

"All we'd need is some sample material and we could storm this town."

It was the "storm" part of that statement that had me worried. I suggested that if we decided to give it a shot maybe we could use some of the material I had already written. You know? Until we could bang out some of our own.

There wasn't a moment's hesitation on his part.

"No. Besides, no one would believe I had anything to do with *that* material."

There was something in the way he said, "*that*." Was it not good enough for him to be associated with or was it too good for someone who knew him to believe he had anything to do with it?

I sensed I was ahead of the game by not knowing. He would undoubtedly have told me had I asked. Kevin never felt encumbered by sparing someone's feelings. I'm insecure enough that I didn't need to hear anyone, especially someone who'd never written a script before, disparage my work. So I just let it ride.

Kevin casually posed, "How long could it take us to knock out material?"

I told him that the *Welcome Back, Kotter* took me ten days.

"We don't need scripts. We just need samples. Buyers don't need a banquet to hire you as a caterer. Just something to show you can cook."

He handed me the joint, then went inside his house. Returning moments later, he carried a pad and pen. He then asked me what variety shows I liked. I told him *NBC's Saturday Night* which had just begun a few months before. It wasn't until after a show called *Saturday Night Live* hosted by sports personality, Howard Cosell was cancelled that NBC renamed their show as we know it today, *Saturday Night Live. I* also told him when I could stay awake late enough I loved, *The Tonight Show* with Johnny Carson."

Turns out, so did he. "Tea Time Movie or Carnac the Magnificent?"

I told him I loved them both. He said they would be our two spec comedy sketches... Kevin exuded that feeling of confidence – almost a Svengali effect. The first piece we ever wrote together was the Carnac sketch. Kevin handed me the pad and then relit the doobie. We were writing together for the first time – sitting on his cement steps. He took a deep hit from the reefer, and then leaned back on his elbows.

Kevin, with a natural rhythm, self-assurance and drawing in and exhaling out a stupor inducing cloud of smoke, began. He magically inhabited these characters.

And with this opening, our career began:

ED MCMAHON: There's only one person who can unlock the mysteries of life – unfortunately he couldn't be here tonight. But in his place, it's my unqualified pleasure that I bring out the Mystic of the East, a Sovereign Sage of the unseen, a knower of the unknown and a man who wets his shoes every time he uses the urinal— Carnac the Magnificent.

I took it down as fast as I could. It sure sounded like a genuine Carnac opening. Kevin plowed on, not waiting to see if I was up to him, pausing just long enough to inhale another lungful of cannabis.

Johnny Carson, as CARNAC enters. He does his patented stumble, and then takes his seat behind the desk exchanging Middle Eastern hand gesture greetings.

ED MCMAHON: *Sim sim sala bim*. Oh sage of sages, seer of seers.

CARNAC: And don't forget Roebucks... They're a sponsor too, you know.

ED MCMAHON: A thousand blessings on your Kasbah for gracing us with your mystical prowess tonight.

Okay, Kevin was speaking faster than I could write. He was a man possessed as he effortlessly continued on, voices and all.

ED MCMAHON: (HOLDING UP ENVELOPES) In my hands are questions that have been hermetically sealed and stored in a mayonnaise jar at the private offices of Funk & Wagnall. So private that even Funk doesn't know when Wagnall's been in there.

CARNAC: Depends on whether he was doing number 1 or number 2. If it was number two, then the Funk will tell the Wagnall. That's an old nomad joke. *Sim sim sala bim.*

ED MCMAHON: We're hoping your mystical powers allow you to answer these questions without having seen them.

Ed hands Carnac the first envelope. Carnac places it to his forehead.

CARNAC: 1492, 1776, and 1975.

ED MCMAHON: (REPEATING) 1492, 1776, and 1975.

CARNAC: (OPENING ENVELOPE AND READS) Name three rooms at the Century Plaza Hotel where Zsa Zsa Gabor hasn't stolen towels.

I was laughing and trying to keep up. He didn't wait. Kevin blasted on, "Ed hands Carnac another envelope. He places it to his forehead."

CARNAC: Mahogany stools.

ED MCMAHON: (REPEATING) Mahogany stools.

CARNAC: (OPENING ENVELOPE AND READS) What's a sure sign you're not feeling well.

Kevin did an Ed McMahan guffaw.

CARNAC: May you fall asleep under a camel with irritable bowel syndrome.

Okay, now I needed time to catch up. Besides, this wasn't writing, this was just taking down dictation. Funny stuff. But I'm supposed to be part of the team. So I insisted I try. Kevin shrugged, "Go ahead."

"So," I began, "Ed hands Carnac another envelope."

Kevin nodded with mild sarcasm, "Bold. You're doing great so far."

I went with the first thing that came to my head. On the radio I heard "Momma Told Me Not to Come" playing so I tossed out the name of the group.

CARNAC: Three Dog Night.

ED MCMAHON: (REPEATING) Three Dog Night.

Then I froze. I needed a moment to find an answer. Kevin just toked on the joint and gave me a stare. As he casually blew a waft of smoke in my direction, I realized I was stuck. Kevin sensed this too, so he came writing to the rescue:

CARNAC: (OPENING ENVELOPE AND READING) What's considered a bad night for a tree?

I laughed. Kevin laughed. But I knew then that this was going to be harder than Kevin made it seem. Something in his smile gave me an uncanny assurance though, so I tried again.

"Ed hands Carnac another envelope. He places it to his forehead."

CARNAC: Mount Baldy.

ED MCMAHON: (REPEATING) Mount Baldy...

I thought for a moment, and then suddenly I had this one. Taste be damned. I was with the master of politically incorrect, and he was already rubbing off on me.

CARNAC: (OPENING ENVELOPE AND READING) What is a gay man's fantasy with Kojak?

Kevin nearly coughed up a lung. "I didn't think you had it in you," he chortled. "This is going to work!"

And then, at that point, the entire world seemed right. I contributed. I was able to do what he did and I was pumped. I jumped into the next one while Kevin just sat back and blazed. It might have been the first time someone actually intentionally entertained him. We were now writing together. My "partner" looked over to me and just listened as I composed.

CARNAC: The Girl with Something Extra.

ED MCMAHON: (Repeating) The Girl with Something Extra...

CARNAC: (OPENING ENVELOPE AND READING) What do you call a girl with the dimensions, 36-24-36... and 10?

Once again, Kevin loved it, chuckling, "... or I would call *her* a well-hung *Mister*."

Kevin created a monster. I was unleashed. Kevin took the moment to commemorate this moment with his Dr. Frankenstein impression, "It's alive! It's alive!"

We had knocked these out in no time... And that quickly we were done. Our first piece of Hartigan & Garber material had been written.

*****

Like a shopkeeper might frame and display his first dollar earned, I kept that Carnac piece. I still have it after all these years. I certainly can't toss that sketch away. It's joining the other items in my "save" pile.

Current score: Save pile: 4. Junk pile: 0.

HELLO, YOU MUST BE GOING

We were ready. It was Hollywood that wasn't.

Kevin had no problems making blind calls. He'd pick up the phone and ring anyone, anytime. He'd gladly leave his name and number, but when you're a nobody, like anybody starting out in Hollywood, you don't get many of your calls returned. That wasn't acceptable to Kevin. So if he felt you didn't know *him*, he would become *someone else* when he called you. Not as confusing as it sounds.

Kevin did a great Jack Benny impression. We're talking spot on. So if he needed to get to a person on the phone, he'd call as Jack.

"Hello, (fill in name). This is Jack. Jack Benny." Before they could answer, Kevin, as the comedian, would continue. "Hold on a second, would you? Someone's at my front door and Mary's at the May Company picking out some gloves."

The person on the other end would inevitably wait. A beat later, the familiar comedian's voice would return to the phone and announce, "That was my neighbor, Jimmy Stuart. He needed some sugar. Unfortunately, he didn't bring his wallet, so I couldn't sell him any."

The call's recipient would predictably chuckle and Kevin would continue. And it always worked, except for one time.

Kevin had gotten Norman Lear, the biggest comedy executive producer in town, on the phone. Kevin changed up the script just a little. This time "Jack" said it was George Burns, instead of Jimmy Stewart, who just dropped by. Of all the people to pick, Kevin chose Burns. What he didn't know was that George and Norman Lear were out to dinner the night before. Norman wanted a word with George.

Now that didn't stop Kevin. He paused a second, then became George Burns. "Hey, Phil, long time, no see."

Norman said "George, this is Norman. Norman Lear. We had dinner at Chasen's last night."

"That's the problem Ted, with getting old. The memory goes... That and the ability to have sex. It's like shooting pool with a rope. Not that Gracie minds – Yeehaa!" Lear just hung up.

These calls continued up to *The Tonight Show* phoning. "Jack" called, looking for Fred de Cordova, Johnny Carson's executive producer and show runner. Kevin was determined to get us in to meet with him and hopefully get him to hire us for staff. Kevin, as Jack, succeeded in getting Fred on the phone.

"Jack? Fred here... How's it going?"

"Fine, Freddie. Any better and they'd bottle me and sell me in Bergdorf Goodman. Look, I don't usually make calls like this – especially toll calls – but I've just come across two fantastic writers who I think would absolutely light up your show – of course they'd prefer you hired them to write it, not light it. But in any case, you gotta see these two."

Fred suggested that Jack have us send over our spec material and he'd look it over.

"Gosh, you know you should do yourself a favor and meet them in person. They're kind of a mix between Groucho and Chinese food. A lot of laughs and soon you're hungry for more!"

"Of course, Jack. For you, anything. Have them call, and I'll set something up. And how about you come on the show soon? Johnny would love that?"

"You hire Hartigan and Garber and you can be sure I will. Thanks, Freddie." Kevin hung up. We were going to have a meeting!

De Cordova took Kevin's call later that day. Next thing we knew, we were on our way over to NBC Studios in Burbank. We were going to land a job come hell or high water.

Well, the tide was about to go out, only we didn't know it.

Before most meetings, I was a bit apprehensive. Considering the way we were "introduced" to the man who ran *The Tonight Show*, I was even more uneasy. From the time we passed through the gate and all the time we were waiting in the outer office, I felt a bit unsettled... I guess it was just nerves. I had that occasional feeling we were being watched, brought on by three separate visits by studio security to the front office. Each time they just looked around, made some innocuous banter with the receptionist, then left. I resolved to myself it was nothing. Just guilt.

Soon a rather tall, dignified, gray-haired gentleman behind thick, black-rimmed glasses greeted us most cordially. We entered the executive producer's inner sanctum at *The Tonight Show*.

"I'm Fred de Cordova. Which one of you is Hartigan and which one is Garber?"

We introduced ourselves, shook hands and sat down across from him. Fred sized us up for a moment, then continued, "And which one of you is Jack Benny?"

He knew. Oh, shit! We were made. That's why the security kept stopping by. We were going to be thrown off the lot. Maybe even arrested for trespassing. Our pictures were going to hang in the guard shack with orders to shoot on sight.

Kevin remained composed, then as Jack, he asked, "What was it? The Groucho and Chinese food? Too much, huh?"

"You had me at first but you didn't do your homework. I directed *The Jack Benny Show* for years. Jack never, in six seasons, called me 'Freddie.'"

I had to know why he was seeing us, then, if he knew it was all a fake.

The producer shrugged and said he had to check out the two "numbskulls" that would go to such extremes just to get seen and get read.

Kevin inquired, "Would you have seen us otherwise?"

"Probably not," de Cordova remarked. He then confessed he really didn't have any openings on staff at the moment.

I was with Kevin who naturally flowed into telling his tales and adventures. Before you knew it, we had spent half an hour with the executive producer. Kevin's ingratiating conversations revealed that Fred had gone to Harvard Law School.

Bingo. Common denominator. Both Kevin and I were from Massachusetts and we bonded immediately with Fred. Fenway Park, Faneuil Hall, The Boston Garden. In the words of a true Beantown native, this was a bona-fide "wicked pissa." We all knew Boston like the back of our hands. Suddenly the friendship blossomed. At least I was no longer afraid we were going to be expelled from the lot.

We three Boston buddies continued our enthusiastic conversation until Fred noticed the clock and said he had to get ready for a run-through.

He inquired if we had any materials to leave him so he could get a feel for our work, in case something should open up. Kevin took out our two spec sketches and said we'd be going in a minute. He needed to use the restroom first. We had evidently gotten close enough to Fred that Kevin was offered the use of his private privy. While he was in there, I was left alone with de Cordova. I didn't know what to say, so the awkwardness of silence was curtailed as I told *The Tonight Show* boss I hope he liked our material. He glanced down at it and saw the cover page: Carnac the Magnificent.

"Carnac. I see you came prepared."

I told him it was fun to write and we could knock those out in our sleep. Then I quickly added, "But we do our best work awake."

He smiled, and then started reading. It was the toilet flush and Kevin reappearing that diverted de Cordova's eyes off the sheets of paper with our material. Kevin held up a book of matches. He indicated one burned, extinguished match.

"Guinea Airwick," Kevin proclaimed, causing me to nearly choke. He continued on, "Carson's right about the commissary food here."

That didn't have as much of an impression on the "boss man" as he returned his attention to the sketch material he had been perusing.

"Wait here." Cordova started to walk out, then returned to his desk, grabbing the material, "I'll be right back."

Kevin asked me what the hell I had said to him that drove him away.

I defended, "Nothing. Just small talk." Then I shook my head, "Guinea Airwick?"

It was probably only ten minutes of waiting, but it seemed like much longer before Fred returned.

"I like it. Pat McCormick, our head writer, likes it. I want to buy it."

Kevin pointed out, "You keep saying *it*. I assume you mean our material and not *us*, like in him and me?"

"Guys, I don't have the budget. I wish I did. But if you can write like this, you can work anywhere. I do have discretionary money to buy some freelance materials. You want to sell it or not?"

"We'd rather have a job," Kevin factually pointed out.

"How about we start with this? Sell me the material – before McCormick steals it. I'll make some calls and we'll see about getting you a job. It won't be here, but it'll be on NBC somewhere. What do you say?"

There was a pregnant pause you could drive a long-haul truck through before de Cordova spoke again.

"Of course you could always have Jack Benny make some more calls for you."

"We'll take it." Kevin had spoken. Boy, was I relieved.

It was a week before we heard from *The Tonight Show's* executive producer again. He called us on a Friday to watch that evening's show. They were going to use some of our Carnac material. And then strangely he changed the subject, asking if we knew Bobby Van?

"Not really. A Broadway and TV musical actor, singer, dancer, isn't he?" I inquired.

"That's the one. Tony nominee a few years back. Works a lot with Mickey Rooney. Funny guy. Nice too. Bone up on him this weekend."

"Why?"

De Cordova simply replied with: "Monday. You're heading to the *Fun Factory.*"

STRIKE THREE, YOU'RE IN

What the hell's a *Fun Factory*...? I guess we were going to find out.

The distance between NBC Studios and the Burbank Studios is just a few minutes as the crow flies. As careers go, it can be an eternity – or a snap of your fingers. For us it was the time it took for ten frames of bowling.

On a brisk Monday morning, we turned onto Hollywood Way and proceeded to the gate of the Warner Brothers lot. It had been renamed The Burbank Studios a few years before, when Columbia Pictures joined Warners, sharing this large and historic studio facility.

The giant edifice staring down in front of us was the ever-visible water tower with the Warner Brothers logo on it. We were there, in its shadow, for our interview with the executive producers of a new series for NBC and Columbia Pictures TV. Our name was on the drive-on list. We were pointed to visitor parking and told to walk toward the water tower, make a left and the offices would be straight ahead.

It was quite exciting being on the lot, seeing all of the other people there and thinking they were seeing us. It made you feel important. There on official business, we included quite a bit of jaunt in our step.

We passed people in costume and wardrobe walking from one stage to another. We became so preoccupied that we missed our left turn and found ourselves at the commissary. Soon we retraced our steps and between Indians, cowboys, monster aliens, and some poodle-skirted dancers from a special they were shooting on one of the sound stages, we found the Columbia TV building. It was tucked next to a sound stage adorned with a red warning light. Underneath it read: "Do Not Enter When Red Light is Blinking." On the adjacent door was stenciled, *The Partridge Family*. That was kind of exciting. All I could think of was how many times David Cassidy, Shirley Jones and Danny Bonaduce had crossed over that threshold and sang, "C'mon, Get Happy."

We finally entered the main Columbia Television building. We were told that *Fun Factory*, the show we were coming to interview for, was actually two buildings down.

Hanging off a wrought iron post two structures away was a sign that read, "*Fun Factory*." On the door was lettered, "Fishman-Freer Productions." Those were the guys we were there to meet.

These two executive producers were actually looking for writers to add to their staff for the new variety series, *Fun Factory*. NBC, through Fred de Cordova as he had promised, recommended us. And, here we were. In my eyes it was to interview. In Kevin's mind it was to discuss where we'd be parking when we started. That's the difference between realism and confidence.

What we quickly learned is that there were five other people also interviewing for the job. So somehow we had to differentiate between us and them. For starters, we were a team. The other writers were individuals. They all seemed to be young, under thirty, like us. During small talk, they each made it known how they had just come off of shows which we had heard of. One guy just finished up writing for Andy Williams. Another of the writers had come from *The Sonny and Cher Comedy Hour* and one of the other guys had an armful of sitcom shows he had done including *Laverne & Shirley* and *The Jeffersons*.

There we were, fresh off of no show. So Kevin let it drop that we had just come from *The Tonight Show* with a reference from none other than Jack Benny, which some may call lying. To Kevin, he'd already come to believe it. So this prevarication flowed smoothly out of his mouth, putting the other writers on their toes, if not deep into their own personal envy space. The waiting area clammed up tighter than a tick's butt in a sandstorm after Kevin's reveal.

We were called in first. Ed Fishman and Randall Freer were pretty young for executives at the time. I was 24 and Kevin's age, early thirties. They apologized for keeping us waiting and asked perfunctory questions like what have you been doing lately?

Kevin turned it around. "What have you been doing lately? I haven't seen such a deep tan on anyone since George Hamilton bought a sun lamp."

Ed and Randall laughed, revealing they'd just come back from a Hawaiian vacation.

Kevin looked at them incredulously. "Hawaii? Last time I was there they had mosquitos so big they could stand flat-footed and fuck a turkey!"

Fishman did a spit take from the soda he was sipping.

Kevin ambled on. "You know, before they became part of the U.S., it used to take six words to say, 'I love you' in Hawaiian."

The producers looked on, mildly interested.

Kevin played off their look. "Yeah. Now you can say it with just a pineapple and a twenty. For thirty, they'll also take you 'round to all the other islands, if you catch my drift."

The producers, when they stopped laughing, changed the subject and asked us what other shows we had worked on.

Somehow, the name Dinah Shore had come up. They seemed intrigued. She evidently was one of the hosts offered to Fishman and Freer for *Fun Factory*, before they chose Bobby Van. So they wanted to know a bit about her.

Kevin effortlessly, and just as shamelessly, shared his experience with her.

"One day, the cameraman came to the director who I was standing next to. He complained that Dinah was becoming hard to light. She was starting to show her age. The director suggested putting gauze over the lens to soften her look. I corrected him and said, 'You don't need gauze, you need linoleum.'"

Kevin continued, "Better yet, just get a gun and shoot the audience. Do them and all of us a favor."

"'Really?' came a surprised female voice that had just entered the booth," according to Kevin. "It was Dinah herself. That was her last word before she fired me on the spot – along with the director *and* the cameraman. I never did get to ask her about the Black baby."

Cringe-worthy is how I'd describe it. But Fishman and Freer, perhaps never having met anyone quite so brash, just soaked it all in. To them it was the kind of bawdy irreverence that they found amusing.

Adding into the coincidence factor - the same director from Dinah— John Tobyansen— was the same guy they used on an earlier show they produced. Hearing that, Kevin instantly told them another story about the last time he worked with Tobyansen. Kevin spent time before we met as a question writer for game shows. He tired of that gig and was ready to move on. The show in discussion was ABC's *Split Second*. Kevin went to the teleprompter operator and handed him a last minute script change.

From the words on the teleprompter, Tom Kennedy, *Split Second*'s host asked: "Answer true or false: Peter Falk, Sammy Davis Jr., Sandy Duncan – If you were standing to their immediate left, could they see you?"

Each of the named celebrities had only one eye.

The audience instantly responded with gasps and uncomfortable laughter. Tobyansen's frantic shout over the PA drowned all that out: "Cut!!!"

That was the last question Kevin wrote. He was fired again on the spot. Intentional? Who knows? But Kevin boasted to these two producers that he collected two weeks' salary and didn't have to work a "split second" for it.

Surprisingly, Fishman and Freer seemed to be quite charmed and amused by the story. They looked at the clock and said they had to meet the other writers but we could expect their decision by the end of that day. If we get the offer, the gig would start the next morning. We thanked them and just before we exited out into the waiting room, Kevin turned to the producers and shut the door to speak privately.

"I see the brain trust you've assembled to come in after us," he told them. "Just a warning. I know them all and I wouldn't put a nickel in that investment. The guy on the end? He claims to be fast. Last show he worked on they clocked him, not with a stopwatch but with a calendar. Oh, and that first guy— you gotta love him, because it would be illegal to kill him – but hire him and I promise you, you'll try. And that other guy over there? Good luck. You can trust him about as much as a slow, wet fart."

Ed and Randall just smiled, shook their heads and then our hands. We were off.

As we drove away from the lot, we were nervous as all hell. Could we get this job? Had Kevin gone too far? If I had finger nails, I probably would have gnawed them.

We didn't have any place special to go to wait. So Kevin, who was driving, just continued on, first to the 101 Freeway west, then the 405 south. As we approached LAX, he pulled off and into the parking lot of a bowling alley.

Inside, we got shoes, picked out a ball and went to our assigned lane. Kevin picked up a few shots of schnapps as he was wont to do. He generally took to drink if he was nervous and couldn't smoke weed. He was nervous a lot.

Kevin would disappear a few times and I would scan the alley and inevitably find him on the payphone. He'd come back and say, "No word yet."

Then he got an idea. The show, because it was a variety format, might be able to hire us as a team for one salary. In sitcoms and dramas a team split the guild established script fee, kind of like two for the price of one. If that was the case for this kind of show, staff written, Fishman and Freer would be able to save money hiring us.

Kevin immediately called the Writers Guild. Unfortunately, in variety shows, the guild had established individual minimum rates for weekly salaries. This meant they had to pay both of us at least the minimum for each week worked. So in essence, we were twice as expensive as an individual. Not in Kevin's mind. His take: they'd get more than twice the output from us. So he called up *Fun Factory* and told the assistant to get word to the executive producers that they could have us both for one fee.

When I asked him what he was going to do when the production company found out that was a lie, he said it wasn't a lie. The one fee would just be twice the individual price. If they mistook the message, that would be their problem. Besides, they'd forgive us when they saw the gold material we'd turn out.

That was exactly how Kevin thought. Lies and deceit were fine if the ends justified the means.

We continued bowling but the wait was killing us. So was the booze. Kevin tossed the ball so hard that it skipped through the gutter on our lane and took out some pins on the next one over. He tried to make those count, but I guess he was drunk enough that I was able to convince him that the toppled pins had to be on our lane to be added to the score.

Now it was time. The waiting and the bowling were over. The clock showed it was 6 p.m... the moment of truth. We had to call and find out the verdict. Were we starting work the next morning or were we going to be looking for a job?

Kevin wanted one more drink to steady his nerves, but he didn't have enough cash. He wasn't going to be denied a shot of courage, so he struck up a conversation with the guy at the bar, drinking next to him.

He asked the bartender for three empty plastic cups. He placed them upright, in a straight line, rims touching. He bet the guy next to him five bucks that he could stand the middle glass up between the other two glasses without the middle glass touching them. "All I need are the items on the bar". On the counter was a book of matches, a toothpick, and a packet of sugar. Kevin tossed down a five dollar bill for his side of the bet. The dubious customer looked at the items; put his own fiver down, thus accepting.

Kevin handed the guy the matches, the toothpick and the packet of sugar.

"Here, you can have these."

Kevin then proceeded to pick up his five dollar bill from the counter, then fold it down the middle, lengthwise. Then he folded it lengthwise **twice** again, making the bill look like a long, skinny accordion. He placed the bill between the two end glasses, lifted the center glass and parked it on the accordion bridge between them. No glasses were touching and the center glass was raised between them. Kevin won.

With his winnings Kevin bought me and himself a drink. He even ordered one for the guy who lost the bet. Then he made his way over to the payphone.

Ed Fishman took the call and gave us an answer. He welcomed us aboard *Fun Factory*. He told us to report the next morning by 9:30, as the host, Bobby Van, would be coming in to meet all of the writers at 10.

Kevin hung up the phone, smiled as he shared the news. For the next 13 weeks, we were going to be working at Columbia Pictures Television on Bobby's Van's *Fun Factory*.

THE TORCH HAS BEEN PASSED

Today was the day. We were starting work as staff writers on our first network variety show. Our offices were on the Burbank Studio's lot. Wow, two Massachusetts boys really made good. We had knocked on the door, Kevin had spread some of his nascent magic and show business had let us in. Life couldn't get much better than this.

Just looking around the writers room – eight of Hollywood's finest, well established comedy scribes, all biting into donuts or bagels, while washing them down with cups of coffee that were provided to keep the "wordsmiths" gassed up and ready to knock out fresh material. A few writers had gathered together in groups, evidently having worked before on prior shows or sharing some other mutual commonality. I noticed that though all were different, they all seemed to be the same. They wore jeans, sneakers, work shirts over tees or a sport jacket over a food stained polo shirt. And all had the same kind of odd look and exuded a quirky, almost neurotic quality. We weren't lookers. We were Woody Allens.

These comedy creators, with one exception – Kevin— all were Jewish. And truthfully, for an Irish Catholic, Kevin was more Jewish than most of them. He knew the holidays. He knew all the Yiddish expressions.

Kevin looked around the room and turned to me, "I guess I'm the 'Shabbat goy.'"

He sure had a way with words, no matter what language. A chameleon man, he fit in anywhere.

There was also something else this human collection had in common – age. They were all in their 20s or 30s. All except one, Snag Werris. Thirty to 40 years our senior, he was an anomaly in many ways. Snag had an unidentifiable accent – almost typical for an old-time Eastern European. Yet Snag was born in New York. So where this affectation came from, we didn't know. But if you were looking for a stereotypical "old Jew," you had found him in Snag.

His writing skills were exceptional – utilized by Frank Sinatra, Lewis and Martin, Jackie Gleason, Milton Berle, Jimmy Stewart, and Burns and Allen. He had performed in vaudeville and on Broadway. He even made multiple guest-starring appearances on TV sitcoms like *The Brady Bunch* and *That Girl!* Basically, if you were a famous name or had a network show, you at some time used Snag's material or the man, himself. Everyone knew Snag. They may not have known his true given name but they knew him in one word – like Cher, Sting, Madonna or Beyoncé. He was simply Snag.

I was so excited and taken in by the surroundings, just wide-eyed at everything I saw. I shyly introduced myself around to others on the staff. Some graciously welcomed me; others passed me over with the arrogance that I was used to seeing Kevin demonstrate on them. And I did notice this: none of the other writers who came to interview the day before with us had gotten offers. So whatever Kevin did or said to the executive producers may have made the difference.

Kevin called me over and introduced me to the old "statesman" on the staff. As I was presented to Snag, I assumed he was the head writer. Snag said no. Some hot shot in from *The Carol Burnett Show* was tagged for that position. Snag knew him, though, from the guy's first gig as a gofer on *The Milton Berle Show*.

"Cocky son of a bitch, too. Berle fired him."

"Why?"

"Berle's hung like a stallion and he loves to show it off. One day the kid comes into the writers meeting before Berle arrives and wants to bet us he's got a bigger schlong than Milton. Then Miltie walks in and hears this."

"What happened?"

"The kid whipped out his humongous piece of manhood. A real two-fister. I mean this thing should have its own area code. Berle looked at it in amazement, then looked over to me and asked what he should do? I told him, 'I'd take the kid's bet.' Then as Uncle Miltie was rummaged deep into his trousers to pull out his schwantz, I told him, 'Be kind, Milton. Just take out enough to beat him.'"

Kevin and I knew at that point that this guy was great to hang around. The stories he could tell. We could learn a lot from him.

Fishman and Freer popped their heads into the writers' room and reminded us that Bobby Van, our host, would be in soon. He was coming in from a USO stopover for this meeting, so make sure we were on our best behavior. Then they exited.

The USO? Snag, a very proud American, said the USO was a great inspiration when he was in the military. They did a marvelous job raising spirits of young soldiers like him during WWII. Kevin asked him where he was stationed.

Snag proudly boasted, "I saw my share of action in the European theater."

Kevin inquired, "As a soldier, performer or a GI with nylons and chocolates for the local girls?"

Snag shot back at him, "I saw death and injury on my left and on my right."

Kevin commented that we might see that same carnage here at this writers' table if they run low on bagels.

The old time maestro just shook his head. He'd seen smartasses like Kevin before, and knew how to handle them.

"I still remember the day I reported for my physical at this warehouse in Brooklyn. We were about 200 young men who all got their notice to appear for their physicals. They had us all strip down to our skivvies and boy were we shivering in the cold. It was like an assembly line – at one stop they checked your heart. At another, they checked your eyes and at another your throat. They had it all moving pretty good except the line bogged down to a stop at a small cubicle that was like a voting booth with a curtain you pulled shut after you went in."

"So that's where they felt up your balls, had you turn your head and cough?" Kevin guessed.

"No. That they did in the open. This was the shrink's interview – where they asked you a few questions to see if you were fit for service. Of course we were fit for service. We all wanted to get over there and get our hands on those Nazi bastards."

It was reassuring to hear, but I'm not sure I understood where Snag was going with this. He continued.

"The shrink looked me straight in the eyes, 'So tell me, Snag. You like girls?'"

"I stared him back and said, 'Of course I liked girls.'"

"Then he asked me, 'You like boys?'"

"I stared him down again and said, 'You bet I liked boys. I loved girls. I loved my country and I wanted to go over there with a rifle in my arms to prove it.'"

"He told me to settle down, everything was fine. Then as he was about to stamp my form 'approved' he saw something. 'It says here you're a comedy writer.'"

"'That's right,' I proudly fessed up. Then I noticed he had a pack of cigarettes on his desk. It was a long day and boy could I have used a smoke. I asked him if I could have one. He said, 'I'll make you a deal; you tell me a joke and I'll give you a cigarette.'"

Snag said he flung open the curtain and indicated the throng of young men out there in line. "'You want me to tell you a joke, just so I can have a cigarette while all those shivering boys are waiting in line, freezing their balls off?' I asked the shrink. He smiled and nodded as I closed the curtain. Damn, I wanted that Lucky Strike really bad," Snag confided.

"What did you do...?" Curiosity had the best of me.

"I did what any other red-blooded, patriotic American comedy writer would do," semi-irritatedly answered Snag. "I flung open the curtain and shouted out to all those young men, 'You can all go home, boys. I got the job!'"

Kevin and I rolled over with that one. Part was the humor. The other part was the delivery. For years to come, Kevin would tell that story about his close friend Snag and the "secret" of how we won World War II.

Moments later the door swung open and the executive producers entered with a very pleasant, enthusiastic man between them – Bobby Van. He exuded a charm and charismatic quality which you couldn't really describe. You had to feel his energy.

He asked us all to sit as he went to each writer, introduced himself and shook hands while genuinely welcoming them to his show. When he got to Snag, he stopped, bowed, then gave him a hug.

Bobby addressed the writers, "This man, gentlemen, is one of my dearest friends – Snag. We are thrilled to have you with us, Snag. Just like the old days, huh, buddy?"

"Better," responded Snag. "We won't be afflicted with the Perry Como syndrome."

Bobby said he could promise us that.

Kevin asked what everyone else was wondering, "What the hell is the Perry Como syndrome?" Bobby indicated for Snag to explain.

"We'd write a Como show script. On Monday, Perry would come down to the stage, we'd do a read through and it would get big laughs. On Tuesday, Perry would come down and we'd read the script with the few changes we had made the night before and we'd all laugh. On Wednesday, we'd come to Perry's rehearsal, only having heard the jokes over and over again, they didn't seem as fresh and the laughter was, for lack of a better word, 'sporadic.' On Thursday, we'd do a whole run through with sets, costumes, props, and there would hardly be a laugh. Perry would call us all together after the rehearsal and tell us apologetically that the script just wasn't working. We'd have to stay up all night to come up with a new show to shoot on Friday. It became known throughout the industry as the Perry Como syndrome. Familiarity breeds no laughs."

Bobby, who guest-starred a few times, said that the staff, on Snag's suggestion, decided they'd write the real script but not give it to Perry until Friday. They'd rehearse with a dummy script from Monday till then. Suddenly the real script was the fresh one. Perry thought they pulled a miracle out of their asses every Thursday night to save the show. He even gave them all raises, including the guest stars like me, thanks to this guy here. "Love you, Snag."

As everyone marveled, Snag humbly acknowledged the other writer's wonderment. Bobby had to leave us soon, but wanted to pass along some wisdom. Unfortunately, it was no less crazy than Perry Como's.

Bobby put it simply – "I want to start out with a big opening production number, then I want a killer monologue, follow it up with a tremendously funny sketch, put in a strong solo for me, upbeat, no ballads, then follow that with another big, hysterical sketch, and then let's wrap it all up in a huge, gigantic production number."

"So let me see if I got this straight," Kevin posed, "you want us to start off big, get bigger, then bigger, then finally blow the roof off the show."

"Exactly!" Bobby opined.

Kevin leaned into me, "And they say I'm crazy."

Fortunately Bobby got rushed from the room and back to his USO tour so we could all get to work. Kevin in the meantime looked at Snag and me, "Start big and end up bigger? That's advice?"

Snag said, "No. That's a song and dance man!"

Over the next two weeks the writing staff burned the midnight oil. Fishman and Freer demanded volumes and volumes of pages. Sketches, monologues, jokes, blackouts and everything else funny that we could think of was flying out of our typewriters. In two weeks' time, we collectively did what Kevin joked was a full season of material.

Only it turns out that it wasn't such a joke. Under the terms of the WGA, variety writers on staff could be paid a reduced weekly salary while the show was in pre-production. Once the production would begin, they had to pay you a much higher rate – nearly three times the preproduction rate and for a minimum of 13 weeks. The upcoming week was going to start production. So we were all excited when the executive producers called us all together for a meeting late Friday afternoon. Kevin figured it would be to go over the first week's shooting schedule.

In a way, he was right. "Shooting" in a figurative sense. It was a mass firing.

Every one of the writers was thanked for their contributions and told they were through. We had been forced, in two weeks of near slave labor, to knock out enough material for the first 13 weeks of shows. The icing on top of that unpalatable cake, we were paid the low preproduction rate.

Everyone was stunned. How could they do this? It wasn't fair. Kevin wasn't fazed. He asked if he could make one call before he left. Fishman and Freer nodded, figuring "what harm could it do?" Little did they know that Kevin was placing a call to the Writers Guild.

Two months later the staff and Fishman and Freer were in arbitration at the guild. The producers claimed they paid us the preproduction rate, rather than the weekly rate, because they only needed us for two weeks of preproduction. They couldn't help it if we were so prolific we would knock out all the material for the first 13 weeks in two weeks' time.

Kevin took it on his own to stand up, representing the writers who had all showed up at the arbitration meeting. "*Intention*, gentlemen," he told the three arbitrators. "Keep that word in mind. *Intention*."

He passionately pointed out that the preproduction rate was created with the *intention* for the writer to be hired for the minimum of 13 weeks of production. Otherwise every show would just be hiring writers for preproduction rates. But they don't. "*Intention*, gentlemen," he addressed the arbiters, then staring at Fishman and Freer, "*Intention*."

With the same intensity of Clarence Darrow, F. Lee Bailey, or even Johnny Cochran, Kevin took a doggedly ardent, yet clever ploy with his accusations. He continued on, claiming you couldn't do a show without a writer(s) according to the WGA's agreement. Therefore there had to exist the tacit *intention* to have each writer who was paid preproduction money to go on full salary for the duration of production, a minimum of 13 weeks. *Intention*.

Then after a dramatic pause, and lowering his bellicose tirade, he pointed out Snag to the three arbitration judges.

"This man is Hollywood, gentlemen. His name is Snag Werris and he is what the Writers Guild was founded on. It was his back-breaking effort— toiling for us, going on strike for us, and opening doors for us— fighting to be treated fairly. Do you want to explain to him the meaning of the word, *intention*? If you turn your back on us today, you're really turning your back on Snag and those who walked side by side with him. You'll be denying history itself, diminishing the existence of this very union. Do you want to tell this great man that his last 40 years were in vain? What should he, or any of us here, tell our wives, our children and our grandchildren about the great struggle? Was it worth it? Was there justice? Think about it. Think about this stalwart man as you contemplate your *intention*!"

With that, Kevin sat down. A visible tear dripped from the corner of Snag's aged, and if truth be known, failing eyes. And for the first time I saw true passion from Kevin – totally honest and selfless. That moment he went from a common *"shaygitz"* to a soaring *"mensch."*

There wasn't anyone in that room, including Fishman and Freer, who could withstand the arguments as put forth by Kevin. The three judges left the chamber for five minutes to discuss the case. When they came back, they had found in the writers' favor. We had won. We were going to be paid for the 13 weeks (full salary) plus the two weeks of preproduction and at *full* production rates.

As I reflect on it today, a cloud hangs over *Fun Factory*. It's sad because what was mine and Kevin's first staff job together turned out to be the last one for our great new friend. It is hard to look back and not remember it as the ending of Snag's monumental writing career, a career which had spanned decades. Now it was over in such an ignominious way. Ageism in Hollywood has a way of catching up with you.

In JFK's words, "Let the word go forth from this time and place, to friend and foe alike, that *the torch has been passed* to a new generation of Americans."

For years to come, that's how Kevin would refer to our start. It wasn't selling Carnac to Carson. It was Snag handing us the baton, and our responsibility was to triumphantly carry it forward.

THE SHOW MUST GO ON

After the debacle of *Fun Factory*, we had some money coming in, but we needed to work. Our "budding" career required our shift into second gear. There was no momentum in standing still. We had sample material and shows were staffing up as this was now May, the beginning of the annual feeding frenzy in Hollywood. Every year, from mid-May, when the networks announce their fall schedules until early July, when all of the shows would be going into production for their September premieres; a bulk of the writing staff positions and the outside script commitments were given out. It was the most crucial time of the year for a television writer.

Kevin and I didn't have any agency representation at this point. My agent had retired and Kevin never had one. Luckily, we had our imaginations which were more powerful than William Morris, CAA or ICM combined. Somehow we had to get our materials read. Then we could get hired. We analyzed the situation this way: we were facing a Catch-22. To get in you had to know someone, and to know someone, you had to get in. Simple, that.

Who did *we* know?

"Doesn't matter," Kevin proclaimed, "We just 'chum' the waters and let the fish come to us."

"And what do we use for bait?" My curiosity was piqued.

"Letters, my dear Watson." With that, Kevin positioned me behind the typewriter while he assumed his normal prostrate position on my sofa. He noted that there were six new variety shows announced for the next season. *Van Dyke and Company*, *Cos* which was a new Bill Cosby show, *The Brady Bunch Hour*, *Donnie and Marie*, *The Jacksons* and *The Muppet Show*. He also pointed out that there were some old returning standbys: Carol Burnett, Captain and Tennille, Sonny and Cher, Tony Orlando and Dawn. We needed an intro letter for each. So he began.

"I'd give my left testicle (assuming my right could function for both) if I could get Hartigan and Garber on my staff! Signed, Tony Orlando."

"If I could pardon Nixon, I certainly can pardon you for loving this material – President Gerald Ford."

"These are some *killer* sketches— Dr. Jack Kevorkian."

"Willkommen, Bienvenue, Welcome to zeh funniest writers since ze fall of Berlin – Henry Kissinger. P.S. Hire them or I'll send Nixon back to China."

"One morning I shot a great script in my pajamas. How it got in my pajamas I don't know... but it was enough to make Harpo sit up and speak— Groucho Marx."

"This material made me laugh so hard, I had tears in my eyes and a woman in my arms. Tell me that ain't unusual!— Rock Hudson."

"These guys are more cuckoo than Cocoa Puffs— General Mills."

"This material put some gallop in my giddy-up – and I ain't just blowing smoke up your ass— The Marlboro Man."

"I'd let them cut me in half to have Hartigan and Garber on <u>my</u> staff— Col. Steve Austin, the ~~Six~~ Three Million Dollar Man."

We had it. Now all we had to do was address the cover letters, put them in envelopes with our sketch materials and get them delivered to the production companies. It seemed to go off without a hitch.

Within a few days, we had heard back from five of the shows. They thought the letters were funny and the sketch material even better. So, we now had five interviews set up.

As variety shows generally didn't have a pilot episode to look at, the interviewing process was more like a sit down, meet-n-greet. The executive producer would tell you about their vision for the show, how much they and America loved *their* star and some of the big names they had hoped to attract to the show as guests. The bigger the names they could get, the higher the ratings would be. If you couldn't get Sinatra, Elvis Presley, the Rolling Stones, Elton John or the Beatles, you had to settle for stars of TV shows or films to come do something unexpected – Orson Welles giving a dramatic reading of Shakespeare in Pig Latin; or Raymond (Perry Mason) Burr as a confused *female* switchboard operator at a busy law office where he/she could never get the names of the six partners right, finally ending in his/her frustrated exasperation: "Honey, just call Perry Mason."

It was the same spiel from the executive producer/head writer at every meeting. They all seemed to end the same way, with the same question: "Where do you see yourselves in five years?"

What a loaded question to ask Kevin. It seems that because I looked very young and Kevin much more mature, they'd always address the question to him. And he would always answer the same way.

"I see myself sitting in your chair, running this show!"

Well, in a business fueled by insecurity and built on a spongy foundation to begin with, most of the executive producers didn't find that a comforting answer. Though Kevin found no harm in it. But I could easily see the abrasive reaction this was bringing. Most often that was the last question and we'd be shown rather quickly to the door.

After four such meetings netting us zero job offers, I asked Kevin if in our next and final scheduled meeting, I could join the conversation, do a little talking. I wanted to see if switching things up a bit might not change our luck. Surprisingly, Kevin wasn't even aware that he was "running" the meetings on our behalf. It just never occurred to him that I was there for more than a counterweight on the sofa. So I tried to convince him to let me at least participate.

This actually went contrary to Kevin's instincts and posed a certain amount of consternation on his part. He always took the aggressive route – keep talking, don't stop. "Otherwise, they may ask a question that you don't have a good answer for." What it really showed was his true insecurities. He was fine as long as he called the shots.

I assured him I could handle it and if there was something I couldn't, I'd give way to his powers of persuasion. He reluctantly agreed.

The final interview was with Chris Bearde, an Aussie writer/producer, who with his Canadian partner Alan Blye ran one of TV's most successful variety series, *Laugh In*. They did similar chores on specials with Elvis and Andy Williams, and then they created and produced one of TV's first Black sitcoms, *That's My Momma*. Chris and Alan had recently split up. Chris was now out on his own and would be running Bill Cosby's new hour-long variety show, *Cos* – The Bill Cosby show. At the time, Bill had the number one selling comedy album. His bestselling albums came out with such great frequency that if you had a full collection of them from just 1970 to that time in 1976, you would have over 20 albums. He was not only prolific, he was hysterical. What a thrill it would be to work with him.

Our interview with Chris was one of the last he was holding for the staff writing positions. He was going to have a group of about 8 or so and we figured he'd heard just about everything already. As much as I tried to interject myself into the interview process, Chris seemed to be addressing questions to Kevin and as usual, he would answer. Since things were going along very smoothly I didn't raise much of a fuss. I really thought that we had a shot at this show. We were very quick on our feet and gave Chris some hearty laughs. At the same time we demonstrated that we had more than just a nodding acquaintance with Bill Cosby and his array of characters.

So it then came to the inevitable question, "Where do you two 'tintookies' (Australian slang for magic elves) see yourself in five years?"

As Kevin was about to answer, I accidentally on purpose knocked the ashtray off of Chris' desk. It stopped the momentum of Kevin answering. As I picked it up, I turned to Chris and said, "Chris, there's only one place we would like to be in five years, and that's right here, writing the best sketch material you ever got in on *The Cosby Show*!"

Chris smiled, called us 'tintookies' again and we soon parted. On the drive home, Kevin knew what I had done and gave me his approval. He realized he had taken over the conversation once again, and he was sorry. Or so he said.

I told him it didn't matter. He is the stronger of the two of us and truthfully, he's the funny one. We drove down Vine Street and headed West on Third Street, toward La Brea. Kevin needed to drop me off at my apartment before he headed to his house. We didn't say much more on the way. There was sort of a satisfied feeling from the meeting and talk might only have ruined it.

When I got home my wife told me I had received a call from a Chris something or other. "I couldn't understand him because he spoke funny, with a strong accent." She went on, "He wanted to know who represented his 'tin tushies'? What's a tin tushy?" she innocently inquired.

You have to realize that English is my wife's second language, so to an Israeli, I could see her misunderstanding of the word. After all, she's the same woman who referred to the Salvation Army as the "Starvation Army." To her, furniture was "phony-chairs" even if it was just a single seat or a sofa.

I told my wife this was good news and I'd be right back. I rushed out the front door and luckily caught Kevin before he left. He was busy rolling a joint for the ride home. I told him about the call and he came inside and we dialed up Chris. When he got on the phone I told Chris it was his two "Tintookies" calling. He congratulated us, welcoming his newest staff members on board. In two weeks we'd start on *Cos*, Bill Cosby's show.

From that day on, Kevin constantly reminded me that we got the job because of my answer to the "where do you see yourself in five years?" question. We modified that answer many times after that in ensuing interviews, and never once did that answer of "doing the best script for you" ever let us down. Kevin eventually realized that you can't tell someone you want their job before they've even given you yours.

Kevin lit up the joint, we both drew from it, and neither of us could wait for the two weeks to pass so we could start working again, this time at ABC Vine Street Studios.

THE *COS* OF IT ALL

Beware of what you wish for...

Never was that truer than on *Cos*, the new Bill Cosby show. When the new television schedule for the 1976-77 season was announced, there were a few highly anticipated shows – series that had "sure hit" written all over them. These were the network darlings. TV critics and pundits alike chose them over all others. They were "heavenly ordained."

Sometimes it was scheduling – the timeslot or day of the week it was on – that would assure a show's success. Some shows were protected by placing them in what the industry referred to as a "hammock," airing them between two established hit shows, sure to deliver an audience. Other times it relied purely on star power. No matter how or why a show got tagged a sure hit, *Cos* was one of them. If it was a music single listed on Billboard Magazine's top 100 chart, there would have been a bullet next to it.

Analyzing the series, you could say it had everything going in its favor. It was a family variety show that was to star one of the biggest, most popular names in entertainment – Bill Cosby. He had nearly two dozen hit comedy albums under his belt. He was a major headliner at the Hilton in Las Vegas and he had previously starred in the very successful, *I Spy* TV series.

Bill was an anomaly. He was one of a handful of Black comedians who had crossed color lines to be accepted for his talent, not rejected by racism. The others included Redd Foxx, Richard Pryor and to some extent Jackie "Moms" Mabley. They were a bit less mainstream – perhaps even a bit too "blue" or abrasive for some audiences, yet they had multi-racial followings.

Bill was straight down the middle and his humor was easily accepted by white America. He never really told jokes. He was a raconteur, sharing everyday experiences via his many character voices. Through those personas, he said what people were really thinking... not necessarily the politically correct view of things. Those thoughts came from the imagination of his characters, while he stayed the course and was always the victim of life's circumstance. He was the "everyman" – not just the Black "everyman."

Our time slot was plum. We'd open Sunday nights at 7 PM, followed by two established top-ten hit shows, *The Six Million Dollar Man* and the hugely popular *ABC Sunday Night Movie*. To give us a further shot in the arm, we were playing opposite a sporadically airing, but ever low-rated newsmagazine program on CBS. If that weren't enough, NBC tossed us a lob by keeping the somnambulant *The Wonderful World of Disney* in its dust-collecting time slot against us.

With all that going our way, executive producer Chris Bearde was able to assemble some of the top writing talent for this promising series. Everyone wanted in on this show. Being a member of this staff, we felt like Jimmy Cagney in *White Heat* when he shouted, "Made it, Ma! Top of the world!"

Among the array of talents at the writers' table was Sandy Harmon, who had just won an Emmy for writing *The Dick Cavett Show*. Buzzy Linhart, who wrote Bette Midler's hit song "(You Got to Have) Friends," and also starred in the cult classic movie, *The Groove Tube*, was on board as well. In addition, joining us was the young writing team of Gina Goldman and Stu Bloomberg. Stu would later go on to become president of the ABC Network. The other writing team was Tom Moore (six Emmy nominations, three wins) and Jeremy Stevens (nine time Emmy nominee, three time winner). Add show runner Chris (nine time Emmy nominee, one win) to the table, along with Kevin and I, and we were the *Cos* nine. That was quite some assembly of talent.

As with any creative group, there was an immediate power struggle. Everything from who got what office, to where you sat at the writers' table. Everyone was angling for a position at the right hand of Bearde. Chris ran the show, but his duties as show runner took him far and wide as well as needing to be at the beck and call of our star, Bill Cosby. That meant someone would have to step in and take the reins when he was called away. The job of "second in command" was an honor highly sought after. To add to the pressure externally, this show was a package of the William Morris Agency. They had a lot at stake in its success, so they stayed "creatively" involved which meant they added unnecessary turmoil to the confluence of creativity, production and business. That should have set off warning bells. Corporations are not funny. They're actually comedy killers, collectively.

Soon it became evident that some members of the writing staff were better than others at the politics of the game. A hunger for power and control was unleashed, and it soon became unbridled.

Kevin certainly was no stranger to that. He encouraged in-fighting and feuding like Vince McMahan at a WWF tag team championship.

Hell, one day he came in wearing a stripped referee's shirt and whistle, just to stoke the fires. Kevin made sure it never died down. For him, with chaos came order.

At our first creative meeting of the writers for show one, Chris told the table that we had booked Don Novello to play the legendary, chain smoking Father Guido Sarducci, a character he made famous on *Laugh-In*, *The Smothers Brothers Comedy Hour* and *Saturday Night Live*. He was going to do some remote blackouts or sketches. On the show Bill would periodically go to the magic giant TV wall and check in with him, finding him trying to make his way to the studio for the taping. No one wanted to take that assignment on, so Kevin got up and suggested we pick up Father Guido sitting next to a guy on a bus, talking. An elderly woman would board, take the open seat right behind them, and then proceed to eavesdrop on their conversation.

FATHER GUIDO: (IN HEAVY ITALIAN ACCENT) ...Emma, she comes a first. Den I come. Den two asses, dey come a together. I come a once-a-more. Den da two asses, dey come together again. I come once a more and pee twice. Finally I come a one-a last time.

EAVESDROPPING WOMAN: Why you foul-mouthed, sex obsessed pig. In this country we don't speak aloud in public places about our sex lives ... And on top of that, you being a priest!

FATHER GUIDO: 'Scusa me, nosey lady. Who's a talkin' bout a sex? I'm justa tellin' a my friend here how you spella 'Mississippi'.

That blew the table away. Chris knew we probably couldn't get it by BS&P (Broadcast Standards and Practices), but Kevin had flexed his comedy muscle and showed there wasn't any assignment we couldn't handle.

And Chris knew it; as did the others. There was one highly sought after assignment – above all others. It was writing the opening monologue. That meant you got to work closely with Bill. He was very hands on with the monologue. That was the job Kevin targeted for us.

Unfortunately, the first monologue got assigned to Tom and Jeremy. That was partly because Kevin had just demonstrated how clever we could be with blackout ideas for Father Guido, and partly because these two veteran writers had lobbied Chris for the first crack at doing the monologues. Chris gave it to them.

But Kevin had a plan. He always had a plan. I probably wouldn't have gone along with it if these two guys hadn't been such arrogant, cocky and in-your-face assholes. They treated us, as well as the rest of the staff so contemptuously they deserved whatever they got. And Kevin was **not** someone you treated with any indignity and escaped scot-free.

When Tom and Jeremy went to lunch, Kevin snuck into their office, stole their rough draft monologue, copied it and returned the original. Then we went back to writing our Father Guido sketches; while Kevin made sure we utilized similar jokes to theirs rendering their monologue impotent. You can't tell the same or related jokes twice. When we finished, Kevin and I stayed late and wrote another monologue, one of our own. It was very different, and damn, was this a place where Kevin could shine. He was wonderful at capturing Bill's inner voices, gestures and idiosyncrasies.

On Wednesday, Cosby made his first appearance at the writers' table. He was joined by musical director and his closest friend, Stu

Gardner. Though Stu wasn't a comedy writer, he had Bill's ear. Kevin picked up on that early. He nudged me, "You want something from Bill, you talk to Stu."

As we went around the room reading aloud our sketches, Bill would take some notes and occasionally chuckle. It's not as easy as you'd think pitching comedy to a legend. That is unless you're considered an equal. And Bill was about to meet his.

We were up next. Kevin and I read our Father Guido Sarducci pieces while Bill was buzzing with Stu. You could tell that he liked them. As I looked over to the monologue team, you could see them fuming. The material we were delivering was "too" familiar to them for coincidence.

Now it was their turn. Moore and Stevens hand no choice but to deliver their monologue which didn't resonate for obvious reasons. Bill just reacted congenially. Chris, of course, defended the material adding that it was the show's first go at a monologue and these two talented guys, Tom and Jeremy, were just finding themselves. Oh, they found themselves, alright– in Kevin's wake.

Kevin waited a beat. He looked around and then, as if accompanied by a cavalry bugler's trumpet charge, he took over.

"Bill, or Mr. Cosby if you prefer, I think you should be honest with us. If something doesn't work," Kevin then shot a look over to Stevens and Moore, "then it doesn't work." He then indicated Chris and continued, "Our fearless executive producer here had us whip this up, just in case... Kind of like 'in case of fire, break glass.' In this situation, maybe you were smelling smoke. So, try this on for size."

With that, Kevin began performing *our* monologue. Not just that, he did it in perfect Bill Cosby meter and tossed in the voices giving it that much more seasoning to a piping hot bowl of comedy bisque. If this had been *Top Chef*, Padma and Tom would have crowned Kevin champion right there, halfway through this golden monologue. Chris was stunned, but he also couldn't say anything after Kevin had given him credit for *making* us prepare this version.

You could have fried eggs on Stevens and Moore's foreheads. They were seething; yet they had to sit there and listen as Bill, along with Stu and the rest of the staff, were laughing – not just kindly smiling. The other writers were agog, comfortably sitting back nibbling on some treats, enjoying a dinner show. My partner was on a roll, and there was no denying him.

When Kevin finished, he turned to Tom and Jeremy. He nodded, then indicated to Bill, "We couldn't have done it without the inspiration of these two guys. David and I just thought it needed a little tweak. Please give it up for Stevens and Moore." With that Kevin started clapping as did the others in the room – purely out of shock, mostly awkward, and hardly generated by gratitude.

There was supreme irony here. Kevin was giving those two guys, who treated every one of us on staff like shit, the credit for the hard work *we* had done. He saw I was none too pleased, but he shot me a leprechaun's assuring wink, and then took his seat.

Bill turned to Chris and told him that all of the material he had just heard for the show was in fine shape, especially the Hartigan-Garber monologue. Chris was part stunned, part relieved. He dismissed the room to go off and polish their material.

Kevin and I went into our little office. Stu and Gina, the other writing team, came in and just shook their heads. Gina, who had an ever-present bag of marijuana in her left hand asked if we wanted to smoke. Her partner, Stu, always perfectly attired and collegiate yet somewhat ill at ease with Gina's openness about her addiction, just sat there in amazement. He'd never seen anyone do what Kevin had done. "What balls that took!"

"I just want what's best for the show," Kevin proclaimed.

Stu and Gina revealed they couldn't get along with Tom and Jeremy either. Suddenly we heard a familiar female voice entering, "You mean those two shitheads?" It was Sandy Harmon arriving; perhaps attracted by the wafting aroma from the doobie Gina had just fired up. She was accompanied by Buzzy, who truthfully we admired.

"When I wrote, 'Friends' for Midler, I sure didn't have you guys in mind. But *now* I do." He had his ever-present acoustical guitar slung over his shoulder like a troubadour. He swung it around, took it in his hands and started strumming as we all started singing his song, "Friends."

We found our little office space now filled with everyone but the monologue guys. Kevin had actually brought us all together with his bold subterfuge. There was no better feeling than that camaraderie. Every face carried a smile. Every thought was pleasant. It's what we dreamed writing on staff would be like.

But then nothing, especially the good times, lasts forever.

Our musical interlude and giggles were broken up when Stu Gardner knocked and came in. He said Bill wanted a word – so everyone got up. Stu then added, pointing to Kevin and me, "Just them."

VIVA LAS VEGAS

"Starting tomorrow, you're through here." Those were Cosby's words.

Damn, I thought, shit-canned again. Two shows. Two firings. We were going to have to break that cycle.

We started to rise, but Cosby motioned for us to sit. "Tomorrow night I'm opening in Vegas. I'll be there for three weeks. That means you're going to be there for three weeks as well. You'll write for me during the day and I'll expect you each night at the midnight show. Questions?"

We were too stunned at the apparent promotion to ask anything.

The next day we were flown out to Las Vegas. Stu Gardner was there to meet us at McCarron Airport with the Hilton Limo. We were whisked off immediately to the Hilton International Hotel.

Kevin and I both were provided very nice rooms. Though when I asked Kevin about his accommodations I was a bit surprised by his answer. "I'm not saying the hotel's going through hard times or

anything, but my bedside bible only had seven commandments!"
That was Kevin. He always had to say something.

Cos had the Elvis Presley Penthouse Suite which took up the
entire top floor, some 30 stories up. It had a magnificent five
bedrooms, a private pool and it felt like a palatial mansion. There
was everything you could possibly want, plus all the exterior walls
were glass. You had a 360 degree view of the entire strip,
downtown, even out to UNLV. At night, with all the lights, it was
incomparable. I've never been in any place that opulent, before or
since. It was designed for Elvis and only certain entertainers were
allowed to stay there. Presley and Bill had been close friends; so
he got to reside there when headlining. How unimaginable it was
that nearly one year to the day we were in "his place," Elvis would
be dead.

Vegas was a play land in the mid-'70s ; the headliners, aside from
Bill included: Elvis, Wayne Newton, Barry Manilow, The Jacksons,
Tony Bennett, Barbra Streisand, Tom Jones, Andy Williams, Diana
Ross, Dean Martin and Lena Horne. At that time, you stayed in
places on "the Strip" like the Las Vegas Hilton (the International),
the Flamingo, MGM Grand, Caesar's Palace, the Sands, the
Aladdin, Circus Circus, the Dunes, the Thunderbird and the Monte
Carlo. They were the showplaces.

Bill's show that night was packed and we were escorted to a
choice table in the middle of the room, center. You could see all
sorts of eager and excited patrons. A midnight show got a lot of
drunks and high rollers, so the mix was amusing to watch; old
men with hookers, young married couples, mid-western farmers,
businessmen and conventioneers, country bumpkins,
international financiers and sophisticated society. They were all
there sitting shoulder to shoulder in the sold-out main room. We
had already eaten dinner; when complimentary champagne was
delivered to our table. Kevin made a quick run to the rest room. I

know that the trip was more likely to fire up a doobie and get ready for the show.

After the performance, Stu showed Kevin and me the way backstage to Bill's private dressing room. We were told this was the route we were to take each evening after the show to meet up with Bill.

He welcomed us, and wanted to know how we were adjusting and what we thought of the show. To be alone on stage, for better than 90 minutes, just him and a chair, talking and making everyone laugh hysterically was utter amazement. Bill Cosby was a master of his game and his act was mesmerizing.

As we quickly learned, Bill had certain sets of material which he performed in each and every show. There were stories about Fat Albert, Mushmouth and Dumb Donald. Then there were his standard sets about his wife and kids. Sometimes he'd get on roll, talking about a mundane everyday event and magically turn that into 20 minutes of new material. It was slowly added to the repertoire and that's where we came in.

Our job was to write material for Cos during the day, send it to him via Stu during late afternoon and then we were free until show time. The third night we were there, it happened. We recognized Bill was using one of our joke stories.

As we listened, the two of us nervously broke into a cold, flop sweat until we heard the audience reaction. It seemed like an eternity as he told the tale, and we waited to see if we would bomb or hit a home run.

"This morning," Bill began, "as I was going for my daily jog, I passed the front desk and heard an argument. A newlywed couple was checking out of the hotel after their honeymoon. When the bill was presented, a small disagreement broke out.

"'What is this item...$200 for a meal?' inquired the groom. 'We never made it to your dining room.'"

"'I understand sir,' replied the manager, 'but the wedding package included meals and the food was there for you. If you didn't use it, it's not our fault.'"

"'In that case,' countered the groom, 'we are totally and completely even... because you owe me $200 for making love to my wife!

"'But, sir, I never touched your wife!' protested the manager.'"

"'Well, she was there for you,' said the groom. 'If you didn't use her, it's not my fault!!'"

It killed. We were exhilarated. That shared look between us that we two had come up with that huge a laugh was indescribable. We went from confident to now bordering on the edge of cocky. We couldn't wait to rush backstage to see Bill after the show.

We made the walk to his dressing room with a bounce in our step. Kevin looked at Bill and Stu and gave a "so what did you think," shrug. Bill smiled.

"I got nothing to say to you guys except keep sending me more stuff like that."

Bill then introduced us to Andy Williams who was performing down the street at Caesars. He and a very attractive young woman he was dating had stopped backstage to say hello. Kevin couldn't help himself. He saw William's buxom girlfriend was wearing a sweatshirt with "Guess" written on the front of it. As he shook her hand, he asked, "Implants?"

My jaw dropped. Kevin shrugged, "What? It says, 'Guess'."

Cosby, Williams and Gardner cracked up. So did Andy's pretty lady

Kevin's inquisitive and dubious mind played right into Bill's inner self. He mastered observation and coupled it with twisted logic. The next day we sent Bill shorter pieces, realizing that he would spin them into his own stories. A few good set-ups and punch lines and he was good to go.

Interestingly, the last piece we ever did for Mr. Cosby in Vegas is one he still dusts off from time to time – "Budget Motel Catch Phrases" he and his wife have come across over their travels:

-Because you deserve better than the back seat of some car.

-If we'd known you were staying all night, we'd have changed the sheets.

-Sure, you could stay someplace nicer, but then you wouldn't have money left over for a hooker.

-Some places will leave the lights on for ya. We'll leave out the Lysol!

-Cheap Sleep. Not just for nooners anymore.

-Thanks to the bedbugs, you'll never sleep alone.

-Millions have come in here... Why shouldn't you?

As a reward for being such dedicated employees, Bill arranged for us all to go out on Lake Havasu one afternoon on the Hilton Yacht, about 130 feet of luxury and decadence. We cruised by the magnificent structure of Hoover Dam, and then continued all around the massive lake. As we dropped anchor prior to lunch, we exited the salon and sat on the aft deck to take in some sun. Before long we heard a minor disturbance, some strange splashing sounds. There were other boats out on the lake, but this didn't sound like water lapping on the hull of our vessel. This sounded "smaller," more intimate.

Our collective curiosities got the best of us. We looked over the side and there we saw it. Swimming toward us was a mermaid.

This was not just a mermaid – it was a beautiful, totally naked, glistening in the sun mermaid with the most amazing set of... eyes. What a body! Suddenly, this stunning, "pinch me, I'm dreaming" moment was broken by a male voice from elsewhere in the water calling out, "Can you toss us a ladder?"

Bill just shook his head and yelled back, "You got it, Herb."

Herb? Who's Herb? And what's he doing in the company of a mermaid in the middle of Lake Havasu?

As the mermaid, who turned out to be a gorgeous 22-year-old Hollywood actress, climbed on board, she was followed by Herb. Herb Karp was a hotshot, 28-year-old, William Morris agent. He was from the new, young Hollywood, wunderkind agent mold. He too was stark naked and from the looks of things, the water must have been pretty cold. He and his actress client were in Vegas, heard Bill was out on the Hilton yacht and decided to surprise him.

Stu tossed each of them Hilton robes which they put on, and then joined us for lunch. Bill introduced us to Herb, who we found in a mere few moments to be a truly charming and off-beat, free spirit. He was a Zen follower, had finished up his Werner Erhard EST training recently and was the kind of marcher to a different drum beat than we had ever come across – certainly not as an agent.

We talked over lunch, and Herb clearly knew who we were. He brought up that he represented the *Cos* show for William Morris.

He'd been making daily visits to the Hollywood production offices. It was there that he had heard rumors of our existence, mostly tales, of how we pulled off the monologue stunt.

"And when Bill told me you didn't have any representation…" Herb paused.

"Wait," Kevin stopped him, "What was that?"

It seems Bill found out we didn't have agents and wanted us to sign with William Morris. If we did, Bill would be saved money. Our commission would be eaten by the package fee the agency would be getting. So this whole "reward for being good employees" was starting to smell to us like a scam by Cosby. It was a setup.

So Herb put the push on. He did the hard sell. Kevin and I were actually thrilled. We wanted to be with a big name agency that handled the world's top talent, but did we want this guy, young, free-spirited and naked out there representing us?

Yeah.

Kevin always had a hard time taking "yes" for an answer. So, he turned to Cosby, "You're a big name, Bill. How much do you pay Morris?"

Cosby smiled, "they usually get 10%."

"I'm asking what you, Bill Cosby, pay."

The comedian grudgingly replied, "7.5%."

Kevin looked at Karp and said, "If it's good enough for Cos, it's good enough for us! Seven and a half and you've got a deal."

Herb shrugged, "Deal." That deal stayed in place for the rest of our team's run.

Soon after, we all returned to Hollywood to begin shooting the show. Back in the office, we realized quickly that the other writers resented having to work on sketches while we were writing nightclub material in that desert playground. Bill and Stu Gardner knew us better than the other staff and would always acknowledge us over the presence of the rest of them. It really put us in an uncomfortable situation.

You've heard of a car that's not running on all cylinders? Our show was a V-8 firing on a mere four pistons. Chris, during the time we were gone, had somehow misplaced his comedy compass. The show, instead of being more cutting edge like his *Laugh-In* series, had become too familiar and way too soft.

Our first episode aired Sunday, September 19th. *Cos* didn't do very well, but won its time slot. Hopefully the next outing the show would do better based on word of mouth.

The next week was a long week. We were going to be shooting show number five, and we just didn't hit stride. Kevin had some very funny, crazy ideas for promotions, but the network thought they were too outrageous. They said we were to "stay on the reservation" which translated meant "don't push the envelope. Don't try to save the show."

The second show aired and the writing was on the wall in big, bold letters. We were a f-l-o-p, an unmitigated flop. That week we came in 96th out of 95 shows. How was that possible? There was a half hour re-elect Jerry Ford paid commercial. Even it beat us!

What was more interesting was the show that came in first that week. It was the little news show that CBS had opposite us on Sunday nights. In the past it had only been a series of sporadic news specials put on to fulfill the FCC mandate for public affairs programming requirements. Now it was weekly and suddenly a hit. It was called, *60 Minutes*.

After our third airing, we held down the basement with our ratings again. At the same time, *60 Minutes* was in the top ten shows, a position it would hold for the next ten years. Kevin immediately contacted CBS via letter, asking them to send us a thank you note or more preferably a generous gift for giving them the newest hit in the Nielson Ratings.

Cos played out its first nine episodes of a 13 episode order. Then word, and the curtain, came down. Everyone was laid off. Now only ghosts and faded memories inhabited what was earlier a bright and proud start. Alas, the bell rang one final time on that once brief shining moment that to us was "Camelot."

BABY, WHO'S GOT YOUR BACK?

"Where's the Funny?" That's the sign I just discovered, tucked in the bottom of a box I was cleaning out. I couldn't believe I still had it after all these years, but here it was. That's what our old boss, Lila, used to hold up when someone would come in to pitch a story. She wasn't overly concerned with originality. She was overwrought with making sure there was a block comedy scene in every show, generally in the second act. A block comedy scene is one where all hell breaks loose, usually involving the entire cast. With us she never had to ask, it was what we were known for. We might be deficient in heart, treacle and emotion, but never in jokes.

When we worked for Lila, you knew you were in trouble if she held up her "where's the funny?" sign she kept stored behind her desk. If you got it, your pitch was doomed. You can't believe how intimidating that was to potential writers on *Baby, I'm Back*. It's almost like making a heart-wrenching, impassioned plea to someone and at the end with your soul laid bare, you're asked, "And your point is...?"

Lila held true to her word – a little extortion goes a long way. She made us story editors on her new CBS sitcom, *Baby, I'm Back.* Due to little lead time, just four weeks where eight was customary, we had to hit the ground running. There would be little time for any mistakes. Lila put a lot of responsibility on her small staff. Most important among those was Mort Lachman. He and Lila were "partners" in more than just a writing sense. He was a legend and executive producer, along with Norman Lear and Bud Yorkin on *All In The Family*. Though he was a co-creator with Lila on this *Baby, I'm Back*, most of his time was spent working on *All in the Family*.

The concept of this comedy, *Baby, I'm Back* had some obstacles to overcome. It was about a Black independent woman, (Denise Nicholas who starred in a sitcom called *Room 222*) whose husband (Demond Wilson who starred as Lamont, the son, on *Sanford and Son*) faked his death five years earlier. This left the main character and her two children (Tony Holmes was the son; Kim Fields, who would later star in *The Facts of Life*, played the daughter) abandoned. The husband returned, having turned his life around, and wanted his old family back. To add complication to the mix, he faced the further obstacle of another man who had moved into his wife's heart. Rounding out the cast was Helen Martin, best remembered to audiences for her co-starring role years later on the long running sitcom, *227*.

This was hardly a "comfortable concept" for either the network or the Black community, which was trying to be enlightening while trying to dispel unflattering stereotyping. None-the-less, CBS boldly gave the go ahead to Lila and Mort's edgy idea. The casting of Demond was certainly a great part of it. *Sanford and Son* had been hugely successful. While his character of Lamont and the moniker "Dummy" haunted him the rest of his career; it also opened some doors as well.

It's not the easiest thing to go out in public and have everyone recognize you and call out, "Hey Dummy!" That's what TV stereotyping can do to you. Sometimes it's the price you pay for success. Some take it as a compliment. Others, like Demond developed great anger and bitterness. He was not amused by that recognition. Ironically, Demond would go on to not only clean up his life, but to become a great husband, father (to six) and an ordained minister.

Before long, we plowed through the first couple of scripts without much difficulty. Some episodes were stronger than others, but Lila and her boyfriend, Mort, would give notes. Then we'd fix whatever was bothering them.

At one impasse though, Lila and Mort got into a shouting match which was quite volatile. Kevin interceded when he whispered into Lila's ear, "If you truly want to get even with him, marry him and you will really make his life miserable."

Coming from the explosive writing staff on *Cos*, this show seemed like a vacation. The staff for the most part got along with one another. We didn't spend a lot of time together in the writers' room. With our rushed preproduction schedule, we had scripts to pound out. We would do that in our individual offices. Most of the meetings with outside writers Lila would take alone or together with Mort.

About four days after getting a story outline approved for our first episode, we handed in the script. Within an hour, Lila called us into her office. We knew she'd love it and probably get us going on script two. Instead she stared at us with a contemptuous look.

She held up our script and asked us, "What's this?"

At least it wasn't her sign, "Where's the funny?"

I responded, "That's our script."

Kevin corrected, "Our funny script!"

Lila saw it differently. She tossed it in the nearby trash can. She said, "Every line is a joke. Every line! Where's the character? Where's the emotion?"

Kevin replied, "On less successful shows. The shows people don't watch. We are doing a comedy you know?"

If looks could kill, she'd have taken out an entire army. "Go write me something I can shoot!"

In a few days' time, I had redrafted our script using some of the jokes we had written, but we made much more of the traditional dialogue set-ups and punch lines. We then turned it in. Substantially it was the same...only half as many jokes. Lila called us in again and we were prepared for anything this time.

She loved it and Kevin had her convinced the first script was a prank. She reluctantly acknowledged her amazement that we could actually craft a full script every line was a joke. Even when someone could respond with a simple "Yes," we had the line tagged with a "blow" (writers' slang for punch line). We just let her go on thinking we were playing with her. When the other scripts came in, they paled in comparison to ours in the humor department. So Lila gave them to us to "punch up" while everyone else went off to come up with new ideas.

The process for producing a sitcom was a bit different from variety staff work. We writer/producer/story editors would all gather on Monday morning with the cast and the director for the "table read." The actors would read aloud that week's episode which we would shoot in front of a live audience Friday night.

We'd take notes as to what jokes worked, which ones didn't. Then we'd go off and fix them.

Also in attendance would be some network program executives who, after the show was read, would give the official "network" notes and express any concerns they may have. They'd comment on scenes that seemed flat or a joke that didn't work. Our job was to fix it up while the cast went off to the stage and started rehearsing. The truth is, the network input was usually coming from young, novice executives who had no real experience. Their notes were lower down on our "to do" list than if they came from Lila or Mort.

Lila was wonderful with these sycophants. She knew how to deal with them. They'd be gone and out of our hair in no time. Kevin was especially helpful in tossing out an off-the-top-of-his-head replacement joke or a humorous run that supplanted something that didn't seem particularly strong. He was much faster on his feet than anyone else there. He'd riff something out that would make the network execs laugh (or even sometimes blush), and they'd leave us alone for the most part.

Lila was quite good at handling the cast as well. They were wonderful and really treated us very respectfully – they appreciated what we did. They knew that if they were on our good side, chances are they'd get stronger jokes in the scripts. As time went on, we found we were getting more and more input from our male lead. Soon he went from Demond to Demand to just plain old, Demon.

Demond was a TV star at that time. He was also *Jet* magazine's "Angry Black Man of the Year." He was none-too-pleased that his show was being written by whites. He felt they didn't "dig" him or his people. He didn't want to be doing what he called, "shuck and jive." He wanted shows to be issue-orientated, angry and defiant.

Not a great mix for network comedy. You have to keep in mind that there were very few "Black" sitcoms on the air at this time. Lila did her best to keep him under control. When she had problems, she'd pull me and Kevin over and ask us to chat him up, keep him happy.

Why us?

Kevin grew up in a predominantly Black section of Boston – Dorchester or Dawchestahh if you came from those parts. Where he grew up, the Irish were the white Blacks. He "felt" their vibe, and being as adaptable as he was and observant of the Black experience, he could generally make some remark that would pacify or humor Demond.

"Chill, Demond. You're as nervous as a 'Brother' bein' taken to an auction,'" Kevin would offer.

"Not funny, man," Demond would grumble. "How can you talk to me that way? I should kill you." Demond probably could have, too.

"You won't because we're too alike. That's the kind of shit they used to talk about us Irish back in Boston growing up. But we slowly integrated when we dropped the anger. We got better than the rest of them who sought to keep us down. You and me, Demond, we see things that same way. What do you call 100 network executives on the bottom on the sea?" Off of Demond's confused expression Kevin would snicker, "A good start."

It always worked. He had a way to calm this guy down. My way was to stay clear.

Being witness to this over and over again, I can tell you that it was no easy task. There was only one person who could pull it off—my partner. He would further put our star at ease equating being the

only "Mick" in a room full of "Sheenies" as sharing the same kind
of social experience as Demond. Kevin would add, "Look at it this
way, where else you gonna find Jews throwing money at you like
this without a gun in your hand?"

When Demond would be upset over some new joke changes sent
down to the stage that the star didn't want to do, Kevin would
just smile at him, knowingly. That usually would do the trick.

Demond needed constant coddling. Denise didn't need anything.
She was so giving and gracious. While some actors or actresses
will "tank" a joke they don't like so you'll change it, Denise gave it
more than 100%, hoping she could make it work. Most of the time
she could. She was the consummate professional for the show
and to her young co-stars. Kim Fields, all of maybe 5 years old at
the time, learned how to behave from two great women, Denise
and Kim's own real mom, the talented actress and director, Chip
Fields. That is the reason Kim Fields has had such a long-running
career. Working with her here, and then years later on *Facts of
Life*, I saw the imprint of her mentors and none of the anger of her
Baby, I'm Back TV father.

When you're self-destructive, bad things happen to you and those
around you. Kevin bore that out. Despite best efforts by bad-boy
Kevin, Demond periodically outdid him.

Baby, I'm Back debuted to very good numbers in January. As a
mid-season replacement show, it greatly improved on the ratings
of the series it replaced. It was so well-thought of by the viewing
audience and the CBS network brass, they ordered up another
season. Now you'd think that news would be cheered and confirm
that what we were doing was right. It would have, had it not been
for Demond. Instead it went to his head. He became power
hungry. He fought with everyone except Kevin and me. He refused

changes unless we brought them down and convinced him to do them. He was alienating everyone.

But Lila was tough and she wasn't going to let her baby, this show, slip out of her control if she had anything to say about it. She made sure that the network never got wind of the pressure on the stage and the furor Demond was causing on the set. Yet some things just can't be swept under the rug and kept a secret. Demond was demanding more input into stories and casting. If this was a brewery instead of a TV show, he'd have insisted on picking out the barley and the hops.

Finally, on the day of *Baby, I'm Back*'s 11th table read, the shit hit the fan.

With the network attending the reading, Demond decided to flex his "star powered" muscle. He didn't like the woman who Lila and Mort had chosen for the episode's small, guest-starring role. He stood up and demanded, in front of everyone, that she be fired. When Lila refused, Demond stormed off the set. The show was temporarily shut down. It took 10 days before Lila, Chuck Fries (head of the production company making the show), Mort, CBS and Demond agreed to finally fire the actress and replace her. Demond had won. And he had lost.

Back in production we hoped everything was now settled. Hardly. Two days after being back in production, Demond was heard in the hallway ranting wildly and seen by a few secretaries brandishing a gun. He was yelling at himself and flailing the pistol in all directions. Fearing Demond might injure himself or some innocent persons, security was called. Before they got there, Lila implored Kevin to try to quiet him down. This was a fool's task. Lila was wrong to pose it, but Kevin really felt for Demond. He knew his pain as he was constantly fighting inner demons. So Kevin intervened. He slowly approached this raving mad man.

With his arms out front, palms up, the Irishman chided, "C'mon, Demond. It's me, Kevin. Unless you're planning on mugging the place, put the gun down."

"Don't come any closer. They're all around us."

"Demond, some folks hear voices. Some see invisible people. Others have no imagination whatsoever. Me, I always take life with a grain of salt… plus a slice of lime, and a shot of tequila… C'mon and join me."

Kevin kept approaching, and now he was just a few feet away. He slowly crept forward and it looked like he would succeed when everyone's concentration was broken by the "Ding" of the elevator doors opening. Demond became instantly agitated again as three security men got off the elevator and stopped. They watched Kevin moving in.

Kevin motioned for the security guys to stop and not proceed toward them. "Demond and I are fine, aren't we Demond?"

The actor's face contorted slightly. It showed more fear and confusion than anything else. He softly spoke to Kevin, "Everything's changing."

Kevin nodded and smiled, "Change is inevitable… except from a vending machine." That quip made the star smile for a beat…long enough for Kevin to make it to the star's side. He reached out and was handed the gun. Kevin took it and set it on the floor. While Demond's eyes welled up, Kevin took him in a bear hug and gave him a huge embrace. The danger was over.

Not wanting any bad press, we were all sworn by Lila to keep this episode (read: breakdown) quiet. Like a pencil without lead, it was pointless. Word reached the higher-ups, and the CBS brass, despite our climbing ratings, cancelled our show. They just couldn't or wouldn't take a chance on such an unstable star.

Here we were, unlike the Cosby show, a viewers' ratings favorite, and once again, we were cut free. Something wonderful did emerge from this fiasco. Kevin proved his métier, his compassion and his fearlessness.

Years later when I asked Kevin why he was so brave with Demond, he confided, "Brave? I was late on my mortgage and couldn't afford the show to be cancelled. Damn if it didn't get axed anyway. There's no winning in life, unless you're a loser."

EARLY BIRD THEATER

As you get older, you learn to expect the unexpected. Yet when it comes, it can still leave you as breathless as a solid roundhouse to the solar plexus. Helen's call regarding Kevin's stroke resulted in just such a feeling. It left me lost. My concentration ebbed and flowed, everything around me took on a different hue.

From books to old pictures to cheap souvenirs, everything I was thinking of junking in my spring cleanup suddenly seemed to be regurgitating thoughts or connections to my good friend. These items suddenly had enhanced value.

Did he really have that much of an impact on my life? Was he connected to everything I have?

Three thousand miles away, lying attached to machines in Boston's Mass General Hospital, the outcome was still unknown. Yet even despite that span of distance, Kevin still had his claws in me. You've heard of the bad penny? He was certainly that plus some pocket change to boot.

Thoughts. Memories. Names tore through my mind. People we had worked with. Studios where we had toiled. Shows we had landed. Movies we had written. Rejections we had gotten. Then there were the firings more numerous than anyone should have to endure.

Was the universe now giving Kevin his pink slip, I wondered? He always seemed to come back stronger each time he was rejected. Maybe this would be another "next time," and he would find a way to triumphantly return. He was in the middle of a new sitcom script when he and I had last chatted. He'd certainly not leave us hanging with a half-finished piece of his magical illusion. The ham that he was, surely he'd hang around long enough for that final round of applause, wringing out that last laugh and taking a triumphant bow. This was his nectar of the Gods.

I lied down on my couch, stared skyward and just let my feelings and emotions flow. I thought of how Kevin never sat behind a typewriter in all those years we worked together. During our reign, there were no computers for personal use. You'd spend days typing and retyping scripts. A rewrite meant you had to use white out, cut and paste (by using scissors and tape) or adding "A" and "B" pages. It all seemed so long ago. Smith Corona. Hermes. IBM Selectric.

In the corner of my office, under some piles of collectibles, I could make out a paper toilet seat cover with some writing on it. I suppose its irregular shape and paper texture caused it to stick out from the pile. I remember well the day it was given to me. It was the first Tuesday of November, 1976. I remember because it was the day of the Presidential election between Gerald Ford and Jimmy Carter, It was also the day that turned into night and then again day.

I remember going off to vote with Kevin. He, of small bladder fame, paid a visit to the restroom before voting. When he came back he had one of those toilet seat, paper covers which he was wearing on top of his head. He had printed, "Ford for President" on it. I asked him what he was doing.

"You mean with this 'ass gasket' on my head?"

I nodded as it looked so stupid.

"It's my 'Reelect Jerry Ford' campaign hat. I don't want to say this election, post-Watergate is dirty, but I pulled the voting lever in my booth and it flushed."

On the way home we got to talking about some of the new and bolder voices that were clawing their way to the forefront of entertainment. A fresh market of young, hip audience-goers was emerging. Irreverent and outrageous comedy was bursting onto the scene, and youth were the much-targeted demographic. Popularity of *Monty Python's Flying Circus*, *Saturday Night Live* and *Second City TV* was soaring.

No one functioned better with "in-your-face" and "without any rules" television than Kevin.

We got to my house and put on the TV. It was getting late and Kevin decided to indulge in his favorite pastime—smoking a joint. We started talking about what we were going to do next. Now that we had an agent, Herb Karp, our conversation moved to what would be the best way to utilize him. We could either wait for him and the William Morris Agency to find us something or we could seek a way to generate activity on our own. Kevin, of course, preferred to take matters into his own hands.

After briefly channel surfing we ended up at some local channel where a late night movie, "Schlock Theater" as we referred to it, was airing. This night they were showing some cheap Japanese monster film that was so poorly dubbed, you didn't need to be stoned (though we were) to appreciate how awful it was. The show also seemed to be constantly interrupted by either the annoying host giving little tidbits about the film, numerous local commercials for some small muffler shop, or by used car salesman Cal Worthington and his (any animal but a) dog "Spot."

Suddenly Kevin put down the lit joint and had a "Eureka" moment. It was that or he had to pass wind. Fortunately, it was the former. "That's it." He pointed to the television screen. "That's our next project."

"Local TV? We're network writers."

"We're going into the movie business. *Early Bird Theater*."

Kevin proposed we write a movie about a late evening's viewing experience. We'd have two stoners who couldn't get dates for a Saturday night, blottoed and staying at home to watch late night TV. We'd write commercials, we'd have the two stoners talk back to the screen while the movie was playing, we'd see them go out loaded to get something for their munchies and they'd make it back for the end of the movie.

He trumpeted, "We could shoot this thing for shit in one weekend."

He failed to consider that just the written scenes would take more than a weekend to shoot. We'd also need to have a movie on the screen for the two blazers to be commenting to. What about the commercials? What about the movie host? All that had to be committed to paper and shot.

Not for nothing in Kevin's eyes. He looked at me as Groucho Marx would on *You Bet Your Life*, before uttering "Say the secret word and win yourself fifty dollars."

"Today's secret word" said Kevin, "is: 'Woody.'"

Now I wasn't sure whether he meant an erection or something else, so I just stared at him, puzzled.

Exasperated, he continued, "Woody! Like in Woody Allen. *What's up Tiger Lily*?"

That was Woody Allen's quirky film that took an obscure Japanese motion picture, which he then dubbed with original, humorous and mostly non-sequitor dialog to riotous effect. It was a very funny, clever concept. Kevin added, "But we'll do him one better. We won't just dub the movie; we'll dub it with famous people. We'll get Jimmy Stewart, Spencer Tracy, John Wayne, Cary Grant, Carol Channing, Dean Martin, Lucille Ball, Robert DeNiro, Sylvester Stallone, Lauren Bacall, Marlon Brando — and Jerry Mathers as 'the Beaver!'"

"They're going to do our movie?" I disbelievingly inquired.

"Maybe not the 'Beav,' but the rest of them will — at least you'll think they did. We'll use impressionists who can do their voices. We'll have a larger all-star cast than *It's a Mad, Mad, Mad, Mad World* or *Airport*."

I don't know if it was the smoke or that fact that it was a terrific idea, but I was starting to see it. The project had three levels. 1: the all-star cast dubbed Asian movie, 2: the commercials breaking up the film along with the host's interactions, and 3: the two "loaded" guys trying to function in the real world seeking to quench their need for snacks. Maybe their car might break down or they might get stopped by the cops and have to talk their way out of it, stoned.

Gradually our casual talk turned into the spinning of ideas really late into the night. It was probably three joints later, four pads of notes taken by me, and after a good two pounds of salted peanuts and potato chips consumed by my partner that I wondered how we'd feel about this in the light of day. Kevin went over to the window, pulled back the drapes and let the sunlight in. We had stayed up all night long and daybreak was already here. So was the outline for our movie which Kevin kept calling "*Early Bird Theater*" and the name stuck.

I told Kevin I'd type up our notes; organize them after I got a few hours sleep. He'd come back that afternoon and we'd call our representative Herb at the William Morris Agency to get him on the case.

"What if he doesn't like the idea?" I put forth.

Kevin's reply could have been anticipated, "Fuck him. We're the clients."

In what seemed like no time at all, Kevin was back. I was still in the middle of digesting and disseminating all of the notes. In a marijuana-induced state of euphoria, everything seems funny and makes sense. When you wake from that stupor, you find there are lots of loose ends or incongruous shorthand.

As I plowed forth, Kevin got our agent on the phone. He pitched the idea for this low budget and even lower brow movie. Herb thought about it for a moment, certainly not longer. He liked it. He said it could work and he'd bring it up at the next staff meeting to see if he could get other agents on board and maybe package it. They'd find a director; maybe an actor who might want to do it and...

"Bullshit! Stop fucking around Herb. Make some calls today. This can't wait!" And with that, Kevin hung up. He turned to me and added, "Trust me, he's on it!"

Three days later Kevin and I were meeting on the CBS Studio Center lot, home of Chuck Fries Productions. In the '70s CFP was the number one producer of TV movies of the week. They put out at least 15 films a year but only in the television area. They specialized in "titillating and sensational fare," titles like *Dawn: Portrait of a Teenage Hooker* or *Deadly Crash of Flight 401* or *Father Ricardo, Choirmaster: They Did More Than Sing for Their Supper.* They just pumped out that shit on all three networks – there was no Fox or UPN in those days. Cable was a place for reruns, not original or reality programming.

We had an "in" with Chuck Fries. We had worked on *Baby, I'm Back* though we never actually saw him, despite his being one of the executive producers. Herb had set it up, so we had a meeting.

We were sitting face to face with Butch Fries, the 30-year-old son of the company owner. This scion held the title of vice president, business affairs. What we quickly learned from our agent earlier was that the company was looking to get into feature films. They were making Butch responsible for finding some inexpensive projects to distribute. He was just the guy we needed to be pitching to. He was young enough to get what we were going for.

Within minutes, Kevin and I had gone through the congenial pleasantries of introductions. Butch finally turned the conversation to business. "So what do you have for me?"

Kevin responded, "A reason for your old man to keep you in his will."

Both Butch and I were stunned.

Kevin plowed on. "If he finds out that you passed on our movie and its grosses go through the roof you can kiss your Beverly Hills home good-bye."

I decided to intervene before this took a really ugly turn. I could see Butch was sizing up whether to laugh or haul off and beat Kevin to a pulp. I explained that we were very passionate and excited about this movie concept. Then I started to share it.

Kevin picked up the mantle and ran with it to the finish line. He even pitched a commercial for The Carnivore's Home Meat Market. "Buy 100 lbs. of assorted meats and steaks and we'll toss in a top of the line freezer." Kevin tagged it with "Some of our celebrity subscribers include Fred Astaire, Leonard Bernstein and Charles Bronson, with whom we have it on good authority, eats it raw!"

Butch was convulsed in laughter.

"What's something like this going to cost?"

The meat or the movie? Butch was a bit on the "large" size. Kevin was prepared for that.

"We figure we pick up a Japanese movie for a song. We'll write and shoot five commercials, all to be done on existing sets for movies you've already shot. We film on weekends when your equipment isn't being used. We get no name actors for the two leads. Pay them 'bubkas.' Then we have a host, I can do that. We get two or three impressionists pick the celebrity voices they can do and we'll write the script. Hell, David can do John Wayne."

I looked over to Butch and with the Duke's swagger I shot back, "You got that, Pilgrim."

Butch was starting to feel it. Kevin had that good old-time religion vibe going, and it was infectious. Butch jumped in, "My brother Tom is an editor over here, I'm sure I could get him to cut in the pieces..."

Then I tossed out, "You must have weekend access to the dubbing stages when they're not in use."

Kevin was even bolder, injecting, "Or else you can just use them and charge it to another MOW your old man's putting out. No one will know."

"This could work. Let me take it to my father."

"No."

Neither Butch nor I saw that coming.

Kevin explained we needed to make sure Chuck would get it. "Do you have any discretionary budget for development?"

Butch used his index finger and thumb to indicate a small amount.

"Good. We'll take it." He went on to explain that we'd get a Japanese film, dub a small portion of it with an impressionist, sweeten it, add some sound effects and then show that to his father."

"How much will that cost?" Butch needed to know.

Kevin shot back with his thumb and index finger in the same manner as Butch had just done, "About that much."

"We'll do the demo and if the old man gets it we'll get the whole project green lit. Deal?"

We shook on it.

Now we needed a Japanese film. Kevin found Shikiku Film Distribution Company. They had the largest inventory of Japanese, Chinese and Korean films with offices in Los Angeles on Wilshire Blvd. He convinced them we were authorized by the Fries Company to find a film to possibly import to the states for distribution.

We screened a few Japanese films at their offices and had no idea what they were about. Kevin felt that was a plus as we were going to create our own storyline anyway. We chose one picture because it was starring a funny looking Japanese actor, Frankie Sakai. We thought it would serve us as well as anything else. At least we were starting out with a funny looking guy. Maybe he would be our Cary Grant.

Editor Tom Fries made a "dirty dupe," an unauthorized copy of the movie. That's what we used to cut our demo. We pulled a few scenes, about five minutes of running time and had Tom on his moviola splice it together for us. We transferred it to video tape and went to the offices on the lot that Kevin convinced Butch to provide to us for our writing/producing/directing of the demo.

In two days' time we had written dummy dialogue for the scenes. We called up our agent and asked him if the William Morris Agency had any voice talent who we could get cheaply. He found us an up and coming comedy team, Roger and Roger, who specialized in voices. Between them they could do almost 50 of the most recognizable impressions imaginable. We made them a deal. They would do the demo for free and if it sells, they'd get to do the movie.

We pulled it all together and in one weekend had done the voice dubbing on the ADR (Automated Dialogue Replacement) stage for the five-minute piece. Roger and Roger were terrific as Kevin and I directed them. At the same time we rewrote and adjusted bits of dialogue on the spot to make the mouth movements fit. We even threw in a few voices that we could do. Sometimes the Japanese actor would speak a whole sentence, but we'd just dub in John Wayne saying, "Yup." We even added some sound effects so that someone taking off their hat would sound like a cork popping off of a champagne bottle and bubbles escaping. We didn't leave any stone unturned or gag untried. We even got ahold of a few local commercials, dubbed them as well, and cut in a few strange, incongruous shots in the background and "hawked" phony products.

With these five minutes, our feature career was either going to shift from park into drive or joltingly thrust itself into reverse.

On Monday morning, Tom Fries had finished editing and adding all of the sweetened effects. We went over for a final preview before we'd release it to Chuck. After some tweaks that Kevin came up with—the addition of a few establishing shots of the house where the two heavy tokers were supposedly watching the show, and some loose voice-over dialogue for jokes—the project was done. Oh, and one final thing...Kevin had Tom tag the piece with a picture of a snail riding on the back of a tortoise that had the snail saying, "Wheeee." That was to become our logo. As a final button, we added the sound effect of the turtle passing 'wet' wind. Kevin recorded that himself.

Our demo was done. Before we handed it in, we showed it to Herb, our agent. He begged us not to let Chuck see it. He thought he could get us a bigger deal at a major studio based on this. Kevin, despite all else, was a man of his word. He used Fries company money. It was theirs. Yet, if they passed on the project...

An hour after turning in the finished demo, Butch called. He had just come from the screening theater where he showed our piece to his father. "The old man watched it twice. You know the temporary offices I gave you? They're now permanent. My father's on the phone now with your agent. They're making the deal."

Kevin couldn't help himself. "Congratulations, Butch. Looks like you're back in the will!"

We were now green lit to make our first movie.

WHERE'S THOSE RUBY RED SLIPPERS?

Lying on my back and wondering about Kevin's condition wasn't helping me much. Emotions were running the gamut from sadness to elation, from hysterical to somber, from plain reflective to mild sorrow. The tiniest nothing and the largest something all held new meanings for me. It's as if I was in a Disney wonderland of discovery for the first time.

Clearing up my office was only stirring up feelings I didn't want to fixate on. Only twice before had I felt so helpless and confused — when my brother died and my father followed him a year later, almost to the day. Then it hit me. They both died during the month of March. And here it was, March again. I know Kevin. If he was conscious, he'd be smiling and saying, "You know death, these things happen in threes."

At least Kevin was still fighting for his life. I might yet get my chance to tell him how much I appreciated him, and how much I loathed him. He wasn't going to get one without the other. Would he have the chance to hear either?

What I needed to keep my mind moving forward was another diversion. Office clean-up could wait. I'd go cruise the Internet, check my emails, do whatever it took to stop thinking about what "could" or "might" happen. So I flipped open my laptop.

I stared at the screen, suddenly thrown back in time once again, back to "*Early Bird Theater.*" While we were writing it, Kevin and I came up with a clever idea for a sitcom. We ran it past Butch Fries who said that CBS, after losing *Baby, I'm Back* was looking for more comedy from their company. We shared *The Thin Blue Line*, a sitcom centered on some misfit marines assigned embassy duty in a South American Dictatorship (think *MASH* meets *Animal House*). Butch loved it and went to his father and convinced him their company should have an overall deal with us.

While we were in negotiations, Kevin found his way into Chuck's office and ended up insulting him. In a fit of anger, Chuck fired Kevin on the spot. Only one problem—we hadn't been hired yet. About to leave Chuck's office, Kevin spied a heart-shaped, brass paperweight. He picked it up and tossed it to Fries, "You can put it back in now. Negotiations obviously are over."

As the company owner fumed, we left.

Kevin soothed things over with the mediation of Karp and the Morris Agency. Within two weeks we had ourselves an overall deal—crafted under the scrutiny of Kevin's calculating mind. Butch Fries was so eager to have us on board that he pushed it through, perhaps without reviewing it all that closely. He just wanted these two up-and-coming comedy guys in the company's control.

The air was still fragrant from the previous evening's night-blooming Jasmine as we approached our destination, CBS Television Center, a complex of sound stages and executive offices in the Fairfax area of L.A. We were here to pitch our sitcom, *The Thin Blue Line.*

As we were now under contract with an overall writer-producer deal with Chuck Fries Productions, they wanted to send a representative of the company along with us for the presentation. Standing in for the production entity was the vice president of development, a very dignified, stoic man named Malcolm Stuart. He more resembled a well-polished funeral home director than a creative executive, but his accompanying us wasn't our choice.

Malcolm knew his stuff in the drama field, but was more of a Count Dracula in comedy. Malcolm could suck the blood out of any joke. Here we were pitching a new show to the network that put out comedy hits like so many Chiclets: *MASH, The Mary Tyler Moore Show, Gilligan's Island, The Beverly Hillbillies* and *All in the Family.*

To park on the lot, you had to be cleared through the gate. Kevin, as the driver, rolled down his window and confidently announced to the guard, "Hartigan and Garber."

The guard looked at his roster but couldn't find us listed; therefore we couldn't enter. Then Kevin inquired, "Do you have a Malcolm Stuart on there?"

The sentry immediately found it. Kevin wasted no time. He pointed to me and said, "That's Malcolm Garber and I'm Kevin Stuart. We're Malcolm-Stuart."

The friendly security officer opened the barricade and waved us through. We had just exited the car ready to enter the executive building, when we heard a commotion. The real Malcolm Stuart, we observed, was holding up other cars while arguing with the guard who refused him entrance because he'd already passed through. Kevin shrugged and smiled sheepishly.

Malcolm was in bit of a foul mood as Andy Siegel, the VP of Comedy Development, met us immediately in the lobby of the third floor. Malcolm put on a good face and led our parade into his office. Andy and Malcolm knew one another, so they made some congenial small talk.

Then Andy looked over at us. "So, who did you bring in to pitch today, Malcolm?"

Before he could answer, Kevin took over. He turned to Andy and said, "Malcolm's got the memory of a fart in a windstorm. If his real first name wasn't Wednesday he wouldn't even be wearing his own underwear. Some people put their pants on one leg at a time… Mal here pulls them over his head until he gets stuck."

Andy burst out laughing and we were on our way. Embarrassed by us, or certainly by Kevin, Malcolm clammed up the rest of the meeting.

Kevin quickly moved on to the pitch for our proposed sitcom, *The Thin Blue Line*. He plowed forward, extemporaneously regaling us with stories about being in the Merchant Marines and upon his "questionable" discharge for the hell he raised on diplomatic assignment. His raconteur abilities were such that when Andy finally stopped laughing and caught his breath, he turned to Malcolm and said, "Where'd you find these guys?"

Kevin jumped in, "Truth is, under a pile of Chuck Fries old clothes. We were looking for a loophole out of our contract and Malcolm was there, also, looking for loose change. He found it too. Where do you think he got that tie?"

Andy shook his head. Wanting to be one of us, the boys, he chirped, "Yup, that's Malcolm, alright."

"Look, you guys are crazy," Andy parsed.

Malcolm rolled his eyes, knowing that generally wasn't a good sign. Andy noticed this and rushed, "No, I mean they're crazy great. I'll buy the show!"

Then he turned to us and asked, "How soon can you have the first draft in?"

"As soon as we revive Malcolm after he hears our terms," my partner returned.

Andy chuckled, "Get it done quickly. We've got a few shows floundering and could use some backups right away."

Once we got to the cars, Malcolm begrudgingly congratulated us. I accepted excitedly, but Kevin cautioned, "Not so fast. We need to come to an agreement."

Malcolm asked what we wanted. "You already have an overall deal with us."

Kevin tossed out a dollar amount that was very, very high, then added, "Oh, and we want to be executive producers."

By now the stuttering and stammering head of the Fries Company looked at us as if we were crazy. He inquired, "What have you ever executive produced?"

"Our career so far. And it looks like we just rang up a sale." Then Kevin turned on Malcolm. "What have you done lately except draw air and a paycheck?"

Malcolm bristled and said, "We don't give out executive producer titles like they're sinecures."

Sinecures? Despite an Ivy League education, I had no idea what he meant. Kevin responded that evidently Malcolm's the wrong person to be talking to. We'll find someone who speaks our kind of language – money and title.

We got back to our offices in no time. We weren't inside two minutes when our assistant reported that Chuck wanted to see us right away. Kevin said, "Malcolm must have told him the good news about our selling the show. He's probably never sold a sitcom pilot in the room before."

Entering the big man's office, he indicated for us to sit in the twin, leather upholstered, high-backed, wing chairs across from his desk. Chuck was indeed happy that we made the sale, but he said that he felt we "somehow" hurt Malcolm's feelings. Kevin responded, "Somehow? Then he's more stupid than I gave him credit for. Sending that dilettante to one of *our* meetings was the true insult... But I forgive you Chuck."

That went over like stink on Limburger cheese. Chuck said that we were under contract to him and anything we wrote during that time, he owned. There would be no negotiations.

Kevin kicked into another gear. He reminded Chuck that we listed *The Thin Blue Line* as an exclusion to our agreement. Flustered, Chuck called in his son, Butch, who as the head of business affairs for the company would know the details of our deal. He was a lawyer by education, but he hadn't passed the bar. Kevin laid it on heavily that it was only the ethics portion that Butch failed.

"Don't feel bad, Butch. With the acorn not falling far from the tree, your father expected it. And unlike me, he accepts you."

Chuck jumped immediately to irate; demanding Butch explain to us that he contractually owned the show, not Hartigan and Garber. Butch nervously confessed that it was an exclusion written into our contract which Chuck evidently didn't notice before he signed it. Soon Butch was curtly dismissed from the office. Chuck asked what we wanted. Kevin repeated the same terms he dictated earlier to Malcolm and the reply from Chuck was essentially the same.

Far be it for Kevin to accept dictated terms when he held the wild card – technically we owned that show. Chuck said it never would have sold if his company wasn't behind it. "All it would take is one call from me to CBS and the deal would be quashed."

Chuck did have a lot of pull. He was a genuine heavyweight in more ways than one. Kevin asked Chuck if we could go to lunch, talk it over, and get back to him by the end of the day. Confident, Mr. Fries agreed.

As we walked back to our office Kevin said he had a call to make. I thought he meant a personal call, so I walked downstairs to give him some privacy. When I returned, Kevin had a big smile on his face.

He said, "C'mon, we're taking a ride."

Our drive took us to Culver City. Among the notable sights there was the MGM Studio's lot. They were a major studio for movies, but were a lightweight in the TV area since the cancellation of *The Courtship of Eddie's Father* and *Medical Center*. It was pretty much known about town that their TV department was hungry. Well famished was more like it. They'd make a deal with the devil to get a show on the air. So Kevin had blindly called the president of the television division and told him about our getting an order from CBS for The Thin Blue Line.

"We're here to save your studio," boasted a most confident Kevin.

Within minutes, we could sense MGM wasn't just hungry, they were starved for product. The recently appointed president escorted us from his office and toured with us around the lot, pointing out that if we did the show there, "This will be your production building, and this will be your editing facility…"

Hell, we were practically being given the entire lot. The home of Clark Gable, Jean Harlow, Judy Garland, Mickey Rooney, Spencer Tracy and "more stars than there are in the heavens." You could practically hear the MGM lion roar.

Back in the president's office after the tour, he asked us what we thought about coming there with our show. Kevin told him we'd love to entertain their offer, and laid out our terms. Without blinking an eye, the president who needed some programming to justify his position, approved it all, exec producer title—all the money we had asked for—everything.

Then he looked at these two happy faces, quizzing, "We have a deal?"

Kevin responded that there was one little bump. He explained Chuck's threat and there was a moment of silence.

The quiet seemed to go on for an eternity. Then the president picked up the phone. What was he going to do, have a showdown with Chuck? Our hearts went into our throats when the executive spoke into the phone and said, "I'd like to speak with Andy Siegel."

He had called CBS and was about to speak to its Vice President of Comedy Development.

"Andy, I'm sitting here with Hartigan and Garber and talking to them about the show they just pitched you." There was a momentary pause, then, "Yes, I know they came in with the Fries Company. That's why I'm calling." There was another pause. Then we heard what may have been the trump card of all trump cards…

Look, as you well know, CBS annually preempts its entire Thanksgiving night's programming to present the special airing of *The Wizard of Oz*, a big ratings success for you, I know."

The president picked up a document from his desk. "Well, I'm holding the ten-year extension of those rights to CBS, awaiting my signature. You either agree to let Hartigan and Garber take *Thin Green Line* (he didn't even have the name right) here to MGM or I suggest you find some new programming this coming Thanksgiving because you won't have 'The Wizard.'"

Needless to say, Andy agreed. *The Thin Blue Line* was no longer the property of Chuck Fries Productions. It was ours. Yet Kevin wasn't quite done yet.

We nearly set a land-speed record dodging late afternoon traffic back over the hill to the CFP offices to tell Chuck that he couldn't have the show. The "Great and powerful Oz" had our backs.

Well, Chuck did exactly as Kevin had planned. His pride was bruised. In this moment of ego driven weakness, Chuck raised the stakes to meet MGM's terms, plus beat it by nearly 50%. We called MGM and bowed out gracefully, assuring him, we'd be back very soon with something he'd love. And the president's final word to us was, "Promise?"

Funny how everyone wants what they can't have, and Kevin knew it.

A NIGHT AT THE BALLET

"Boys..." Chuck Fries greeted me with that and a wave as I passed him in the hallway.

"Boys?" I was alone.

That's the funny thing about being part of a successful team in Hollywood. Along with fortune and fame comes a bit of diplopia (double vision). You see one of us, you see both of us. Your two beings are treated as one in a unified grouping: The good <u>and</u> the bad. The ying <u>and</u> the yang. *Starsky <u>and</u> Hutch*.

We had even lost our names Kevin and David. We were: "the boys." Hell, you could be in your 70s and you were still, "the boys." Once it began, it stuck.

This condition had its perks which not surprisingly, Kevin used to his advantage. He went on vacation right after we signed our development deal with the Charles Fries Company. Kevin was gone for two weeks and no one knew otherwise. I would walk the halls, pop my head into the chief's office from time to time and ask if he had seen Kevin. This was intentional (on Kevin's suggestion). As anticipated, he would scratch his head and say he thought he just saw him heading down the hall, or in the elevator, or better yet, "in the can." This of course would have been impossible as he was in Boston, visiting family. So all went accordingly as my partner anticipated it would.

Then Kevin returned. It didn't take long to tell he was restless. Success had a way of bringing that out in him. He always cherished the battle, rarely the victory.

During that swelteringly hot summer of 1976, I had eagerly wanted to share an idea I had for a new show to pitch. Now that Kevin was back, I could reveal it to him. Surprisingly, Kevin didn't want to hear it. At least not yet. He pointed out that our overall deal with CFP had some built in triggers for automatic renewal-- something Kevin fought for, and got. Now he was having second thoughts.

The way our deal worked was if during the first year of our contract we sold enough TV shows to make more money than our guaranteed compensation, we would automatically be picked up for a second year—with a substantial financial bump. If we passed the third year's threshold in the first or second year, we'd automatically be picked up for a third year. So the incentive, if we wanted to stay for the full three years, was to sell a lot of shows. If we failed to do so, we'd be cut after the first year.

What concerned Kevin was that we had sold two sitcom pilots to CBS within three weeks of commencing our deal—*The Thin Blue Line* and *Local 141*. If we sold one more, we were guaranteed to stay at CFP for at least a second year.

So before we got too far into writing the two pilots, Kevin hatched a plan. Let's hold off on selling more until we need to. Kevin had wanderlust in his veins and couldn't see himself staying anywhere for two years, let alone three. Wasn't that the point, I wondered, of his structuring the deal this way? I was, as always, baffled by Kevin's reasoning. Although, hadn't he successfully lead us this far?

As for me, I was set on putting down roots; having some guaranteed income. Stability wasn't my enemy. Though it was Kevin's by nature. He had no problem with making money, certainly not with spending it, just with having to work for it.

"So, what do you want to do?" was my question.

"Movies. They're outside our agreement. As long as we don't do more TV shows, we can sell anything we want. We'll get the extra money and Chuck doesn't get us for the extra years."

I proposed we table this discussion for later, just get going on the two scripts we had to deliver and see where that would take us. Mr. Hartigan had other plans for what was feeling like the departure turnstile for Mr. Toad's Wild Ride. My voice fell on deaf ears. Kevin's mind was already spinning. His next question came totally out of the blue.

"How about we do a Marx Brothers movie?"

"Well, for starters, they're dead."

"Just technically."

"No, literally. All except Zeppo, the unfunny one."

Kevin had something up his sleeve and he was about to bare it. "Listen, I just saw *Beatlemania* on Broadway. Lines out the door. We can do that with the Marx Brothers."

"The Marx Brothers singing the Beatles?" My sarcasm was pointed because my dreams of security were in this crazy man's hands and I could see it all whizzing past me now.

Kevin "took me to the window," an expression he loved and actually used often. He'd walk you with his comforting arm around your shoulders to a window. As the two of you gazed outside he'd paint some fanciful picture of what's out there below if you really peered hard.

"Look out there. Take a good look. What do you see?"

"Smog and traffic."

"Look harder. What I see is opportunity. Our opportunity. It's in the shape of a contemporary Marx Brothers movie. Picture Chevy Chase, Dan Aykroyd and John Belushi. Bill Murray if we need a Zeppo."

Damn it. He did it to me again. Suddenly I was starting to get it. We could write an original Marx Brothers movie, use these *SNL* guys to star and we'd possibly be growing a franchise of pictures. If *Beatlemania* was such a recognized hit, why not something as classic as the Marx Brothers?

"And it's outside our deal with Chuck. He can't stop us."

We ran the idea by Herb who stopped by our office. He was as crazy as the Mad Hatter but as our agent, he got us results. Kevin loved him because he was malleable—or more accurately, scared of him. After hearing our proposal, Karp was reassuring it could work.

"If you had a script, I could get it to the *Saturday Night Live* guys. They're William Morris clients. We could package it!"

Kevin was too excited. He didn't want to wait. He suggested Herb get his ass in gear and call all the studios. "Get us a pitch meeting—and tell them we've got the *SNL* guys."

"But you don't."

"We will if we get the deal!"

"Give me something to work with; something to show—a script, a treatment, at least a sample scene," our agent suggested. "How long do you need?"

Kevin and I both replied simultaneously, but with different answers.

I said, "A week."

Kevin, as usual, was a bit more optimistic. "Now! C'mon Herb. You want to show them something, show them us."

Herb departed, fully gassed. That left me looking at Kevin. "You realize we have two pilots that we have to write?"

He made his way to the sofa, "We'll get to 'em."

With great resignation I fed a piece of paper into the typewriter.   All my mind could focus on was the sheer insanity of it all. Our pilots would soon be due, now a feature that didn't have a story, didn't have any characters (not that the Marx Brothers ever really played characters) and didn't have a production company to back us. Hell, how were we going to pull all of it off? Not to mention, Chuck Fries would go through the roof if he got wind of this. We were supposed to belong to his company.

"We do," Kevin agreed. "But just for TV. Do you want to work for him for another year or do you want to walk to our next gig with more money than we can stuff into our pockets?" Kevin lit a freshly rolled joint and began. I knew this plan had nothing but disaster written all over it, but there was no stopping this runaway train. And a pocket full of money was intriguing.

One thing we agreed upon, *A Night at the Opera* was the funniest Marx Brothers film. That would be the best movie to loosely "borrow" from. We'd keep it far enough away that it would be an original, but close enough that you'd know it was "homage." He preferred that term to "knock off," or more acutely, "commemorative humor."

Abstract a thought as it was, Kevin asked me for my favorite cities. Of course Boston was on top of my list. Then he wanted to know where I'd never been before but wanted to go someday. I told him I thought Washington, D.C. and New Orleans would be interesting places to see.

Kevin gave me that famous gnome look and smiled, "So you shall. That's where we're going to set the movie. We'll call it, *A Night at the Ballet.*

I started typing as Kevin laid back, drew ever so peacefully from his doobie, and spoke the thoughts he envisioned. "I see Roscoe C. Tinsell – pronounced Tin-sell – lying, eyes closed, on a beach blanket. Think Groucho. He's searching for of a scheme to save a financially strapped ballet company when he's suddenly cast in a shadow."

EXT. SANDY BEACH - DAY

Fast talking rogue, Roscoe C. Tinsell, lies on his back, eyes closed, taking in the sun while lost in contemplation. Charlotte Chickelbaum, a middle-aged, dowager stands nearby, setting out a blanket. Her enormous size is casting a long shadow over Tinsell. He sits up.

TINSELL: Say, Toots, mind moving it down the beach a mile or so? You're causing a shadow larger than Mount Whitney. And if you've ever tried to mount Whitney you'd know that she's ticklish and it's tougher than trying to Kilimanjaro.

MRS. CHICKELBAUM: I'll have you know this is a free beach.

TINSELL: Yes, for people... Whales have their own section. It's called the ocean.

MRS. CHICKELBAUM: Why, I never...

TINSELL: You should try it sometime. You. Me. A forklift.

MRS. CHICKELBAUM: I beg your pardon.

TINSELL: Begging becomes you. So does darkness on a moonless night. That way I could look you straight into your eyes I wouldn't have to see you. Say, you don't know a good taxidermist, do you?

MRS. CHICKELBAUM: Why should I?

TINSELL: Because the one who did the current job on you doesn't qualify.

(HE IS ALMOST BLINDED BY THE REFLECTION OF HER LARGE DIAMOND RING.)

TINSELL: Say, that's an impressive piece of sugar you got there on your finger.

MRS. CHICKELBAUM: Thank you. It was given to me by my late husband, Holmeyer.

TINSELL: With your looks and that charm, he ain't late— he's never coming home. Say, how'd you like to join me? Pull up a continent. We could get playful and spoon. Maybe we'll even have a Hawaiian luau. I could bury you in the sand and watch the kids stuff apples in your mouth. But marry me first. And I'll let you lavish me in riches.

MRS. CHICKELBAUM: I think not.

TINSELL: Suit yourself. And speaking of suits, what is that contraption you're wearing?

MRS. CHICKELBAUM: I'll have you know this is a de la Renta.

TINSELL: You don't say? Mine's a de la Owna. And it's waterproof. I know because seeing you I wet myself and I don't feel a thing. Then again it could just be a massive stroke.

MRS. CHICKELBAUM: You are very brash.

TINSELL: Are those shoulder straps or tether lines to keep you earthbound?

(TINSELL ROLLS OVER, NOW LYING ON HIS STOMACH.)

MRS. CHICKELBAUM: What are you doing?

TINSELL: Turning the other cheek. You're driving me wild. They should build an erection in your honor.

MRS. CHICKELBAUM: Really?

TINSELL: Well looking at you, they'd have to build one. No one would get one naturally.

MRS. CHICKELBAUM: I don't think I like you.

TINSELL: Say the word and let's get married. I'll find us a judge... On second thought, I'll have a better chance with a jury.

MRS. CHICKELBAUM: I believe this conversation is over.

TINSELL: I believe I can fly, but so far I haven't taken off. Look, I can see this is going nowhere. But I must say that I've had a wonderful conversation. Unfortunately <u>this</u> wasn't it.

MRS. CHICKLEBAUM: Why, I never...

TINSELL: Oh, so we're back to that again. Maybe you should. Save us both a lot of time.

"This has box office hit written all over it!" enthused Claire Townsend, the young and exceptionally savvy Vice President of Creative Affairs at United Artist Film Studio.

We, along with Herb Karp, were pitching the movie in the U.A. features development offices. Kevin and I had just performed our sample scene – he was Roscoe and I was...not. We had already pitched Claire the general story in loose terms, but the beach scene was to demonstrate what we had in mind. She told us she could hear the voices, followed by raucous laughter. "Young audiences will flock to this," declared the UA Veep.

Kevin couldn't help himself. "That beats Paramount. Over there, the marketing department motto is, 'If it's one of our pictures, there's sure to be an empty seat in the house.'"

Claire inquired whether we had a production company attached. Kevin took us by surprise when he revealed we'd be aligning ourselves with Chuck Fries Productions. That turned both Herb's head and mine.

The studio exec was curious if we'd brought the pitch anywhere else. Herb told her she was our first stop, but that he had other meetings set up for us.

"Cancel 'em. The boys and *A Night at the Ballet* are with me, here, at United Artists. I'll contact business affairs."

"There is one more thing," Kevin posited before continuing.

Whenever Kevin started out with that preamble you never knew where it would lead. "We need the studio to put up some research money so we can go to Boston, New York, Washington, D.C. and New Orleans. We want this to ring of authenticity. These cities all have fantastic ballet companies."

"Done," she replied. "Let's get this going!"

At the car Herb asked why Kevin brought up Chuck's company. "I could have shopped it around, maybe even gotten into us into a bidding war."

Kevin smiled back, "Because no money on earth could bring me the pleasure of seeing Chuck's face when he realizes that we're going over our guarantee and he can't automatically have us for another year."

I didn't see it that way. "He'll shit…"

"…and then he'll love us," Kevin reassured. "He always wanted to make real movies. Now we got him a major."

During the drive back to our offices, I reminded Kevin that we still had to get the two TV pilots written. "On top of that, Claire's expecting us to get going immediately on her picture."

"And don't forget our research trip," Kevin shrugged.

TUTU MUCH

Kevin handed me an Instamatic camera just before we popped our heads into Chuck's office after returning from United Artists. I stared at the camera with a puzzled look. "Don't worry," Kevin said. "You'll know when to use it."

"I'm busy. What do you two want?" barked Fries.

Kevin was in no hurry. "Chuck, some people—take your son Butch for example—are a lot like Slinkies...not really good for anything, but you can't help smiling when you see it tumble down the stairs."

Chuck was confused by this opening statement, and truthfully so was I.

"When I share with you our good news, I think you might even push him."

Now Chuck was really confused and growing impatient. Kevin truly enjoyed toying and parrying with the boss. It was almost a sport for him...and he was an all-star at needling the big man. "We, that *includes* you and your company, are going to be doing a movie for United Artists."

"What are you talking about?"

"We, this time it means David and me, just sold a movie to United Artists, and we're going to let your company produce it."

"You're going to let me? How generous of you, but you're under contract to me. This time there's no exclusion."

"This time we don't need one!"

Kevin produced and read from our contract. Sure enough, as Chuck had indicated, it specifically stated we were under contract for all writing and producing services for the period of three years—in television. Hear that last word, Chuck, television?"

Fries snatched the contract from Kevin's hands while I lifted the camera into position.

Snap. I took a picture as the reality sunk in. Chuck's expression went from confused to irate.

"You're an interesting man, Chuck. If I told you there were four billion stars in the sky, you'd have believed me. But, I tell you what's in this contract and you have to read it. Where's the trust?"

I'd never seen that exact shade of red that Chuck's face became. It was like watered down borscht. I snapped another shot.

"Hey, don't look at me," Kevin said. "It's *your* son who wrote the fuckin' deal!"

We had done it to him again. He wasn't pissed. Chuck had passed that point seconds ago. He was seething.

"Temper those feelings, Chuck. Remember, you're never too old to learn something stupid. After Butch, how many kids do you have?"

"Five."

"Well, smart guys are supposed to learn from their mistakes…"

Snap. I took another picture. The flash may have been all that separated Chuck from flying over his desk to take Kevin out.

After filling in the boss about the sale, Kevin let up and actually calmed him. He succeeded in getting Fries to start focusing about how good this could be for his prestige in the industry. Kevin fluffed him up a bit, unruffled his feathers and even stroked his plume. We assured Chuck that he'll appear like such a hero having us with two pilots and a feature, all under his banner. It would make him look visionary.

"Now would be a good time to call your publicist and get the press going on this," chided an ever-confident Kevin.

Boy, had Chuck been played. He wanted to know how we were doing on the two pilots that DID belong to his company, now that we had brought it up. Kevin said we'd work on them during the train trip.

"What train trip? Fries was baffled once again.

Kevin explained it was part of the research trip that UA was going to pay for. Then he added how it would help if Chuck advanced us the money plus per diem so we could leave sooner than later— which of course would speed up the delivery of HIS two network TV pilots.

What I found most interesting is that never once did Chuck ask what the movie was about, not even its name. It was all money, dollars and cents with him. This was a very important man in the industry, and he let himself be played like a cheap, Stradivarius knock-off. How could he not even be interested in what we sold and what his name would ultimately be associated with?

Again, money was his main concern. We told him that we were taking this cross country train trip because the movie took place on a train with stops in Boston, New York, Washington, D.C. and New Orleans. Of course we'd need to spend a few nights in each city to do some research.

Chuck couldn't wrap his head around that. "What do you need a research trip for? Why don't you just go to the library and get a book?"

"What a cheap, bastard you are, Chuck. Not even go to a bookstore and buy a book, but go to the fuckin' library and check one out?"

Over the next few days, Kevin took full and total charge of our itinerary. I just sat and wrote. He made arrangements for us to visit with the ballet companies in those cities. Kevin had a few tricks up his sleeve too. He loved publicity and was going to take advantage of every opportunity.

Kevin called upon Chuck's publicist, utilizing his connections to get us on local talk shows in these cities, special mayoral visits, and even a "state department" meeting in Washington. Kevin had this all worked out as if we were visiting dignitaries and we were going to be wined and dined till the cows came home...or at least we came home.

During the cross country railroad trip on the Southwest Limited, Kevin became *los mejores amigos* (best friends) with the red caps—the hardworking Amtrak guys who turned down the beds, got you tables in the dining car and made sure you had everything in your room that you wanted. We didn't have a private car. We did have private compartments with pull down beds, as well as toilets, which afforded us a fair amount of privacy when Kevin wanted to snort up a few lines.

Hartigan loved the club car. He could be found there if he wasn't in his room napping—or toking—or coking. You'd walk in and he was either buying someone a drink or holding court, telling the assembled crowd a fanciful story:

"The other day I was driving my 8-year-old daughter to school and there was a commotion in the car in front of us. It was swerving and braking. Evidently it ended up being quite physical because the woman cut off this guy's pecker and tossed it out the window. It splatted right on my front windshield. It stuck there for a second so I put on the wipers and washed it away. I thought I was okay until my daughter asked me, 'Daddy, what was that?'"

"I was kind of shocked, but not wanting to expose her to anything sexual at her young age, I said, 'It.... it was only a bug, Honey.'"

"My little girl sat with a confused look on her face, and after a moment said, 'Sure had a big dick, didn't it?'"

No one was disappointed in a Kevin tale, especially with a few drinks in him.

"You know the definition of a virgin, don't you? The ugliest girl in the third grade."

Okay, I knew Kevin had enough. Time to rein him in. Next stop, Boston.

SOX VS. YANKEES

We were in Boston, staying in luxury suites at the stately, pricey and vaunted Ritz-Carlton Hotel, overlooking the swan boats on the lake in the Boston Public Garden. In the late '70s and '80s, if you were anyone, you were seen at the Ritz. We certainly had arrived when you considered Kevin's childhood as a "Dot Rat" from Dawchestahh and me being even farther away as a hick west-ender from Springfield. Our five-day stay there was perfect. It allowed us to check out the Boston Ballet, see old friends and family, and catch Freddie Lynn and Jim Rice at a Sox Game at Fenway. Hell, we even squeezed in a little time for writing.

Our second afternoon there, we had an interesting meeting with Senator Ted Kennedy which Kevin had arranged. Ordinarily this would seem surprising, but the unusual tended to become the usual when it came to Kevin and his arrangements. There were rumors Teddy was going to be drafted to run for President. Getting a sit-down with him was easily manipulated when Kevin called his office explaining we were with United Artists AND we were Massachusetts native sons interested in his candidacy.

I had met him years before as a child when he first ran for senator. My father, a photographer, was going to be doing some press stills of him and took me out of school so I could meet him. I reminded the senator of that event. As any good politico would do, he faked remembering it. What I took away most from the meeting, though, was Kevin asking the senator where Ted's brother John's papers were stored. Ted said that the JFK Presidential Library had most of them (he could make arrangements for us anytime to see them) and the rest were housed in the Library of Congress, in Washington. I didn't know why at that time Kevin was so curious about JFK's papers and wouldn't find out until a bit later. Here we were with the great Senator Teddy K. Damn, this trip was really starting off gangbusters.

Our final morning in Boston was to be the most eventful. Kevin had us scheduled to appear on the *Good Morning, Boston* television show. I had never been interviewed on TV before and didn't know what to expect. Kevin was the ham in our combo. He loved it. While talking about being in town as research for the movie, Kevin let it be known that we were local boys who made good out west but never lost our love for our wicked fanaticism with the holiest of holies—the Red Sox. The show's congenial hostess asked us about that—certainly a safe subject to discuss in Beantown.

"So, what do you think of the Sox this year?"

"They have too much in common with your everyday country possums," Kevin observed. "They both play dead at home and get killed on the road!"

That was kind of funny to a true Sox fan, but then Kevin got carried away. The station's switchboard illuminated like a Christmas tree with his next comment.

"During a recent trip on the "T" (Boston's Mass Transit subway train) I got to wondering what you get if you filled a Red Line subway car with the 40 Red Sox players and 40 lesbians? Eighty people, none of 'em do dick!"

I died. And I'm sure I wasn't alone. Had the hostess not cut immediately to commercial, Kevin would have continued on. Only God knows where that would have led us.

From Boston it was a mere four hour train ride to New York City. I had gone to college there, Columbia University, so I knew my way around. I had actually had my fill of the Big Apple as a poor student—good grades—poor financially. Now I was coming back with a bit of money behind me and an expense account. So we did it up right. We stayed at the Plaza and saw a couple of plays, as well as a trip behind the scenes at Lincoln Center for the ballet research.

The title of artistic director to a ballet company is quite prestigious, we were to learn. The flamboyant chief of the Lincoln Center Ballet troupe offered Kevin and me a series of catty remarks, coupled with tales of his sexual prowess undertaken during company tours.

I'm not sure he realized we were more interested in PG entertainment, not the "X" rated stuff. Fortunately we did get to see and hear what a rehearsal regimen was like and what it took to be a ballet performer. No easy task, that. Just watching them left me fatigued. I was looking forward to relaxing at the hotel that afternoon; Kevin had other things in store for us.

What certainly surprised me is that Kevin managed to somehow schedule a late afternoon meeting over at the HBO headquarters in mid-town. HBO had nothing to do with the ballet trip and were not signatories to the Writer's Guild, so we couldn't work for them. Or so it would have seemed. But you never said "couldn't" to Kevin without some sort of challenge.

We met there with Michael Fuchs, the man who was in charge of buying programs for the relatively new pay TV outlet. At that time HBO was small potatoes in original programming. They were mostly a pay movie service. We had read that they wanted to do some original shows and specials. That's what Kevin wanted a piece of.

We pitched Fuchs a TV special—a one man JFK show. Fuchs, a devout liberal Democrat, seemed interested. Our project was one of a number of one-man plays, which were proliferating, built around the lives of the famous: Mark Twain, Charles Dickens, Golda Meir, Will Rogers, even Groucho Marx went on the road as...wait for it, *An Evening with Groucho*.

Though he liked the idea a lot, Fuchs had a few concerns. First, getting the Kennedy family's permission. HBO had tried to do a biographical film of JFK and the Kennedys put the kibosh on that. Kevin told the VP we had met with Ted, we had access to all of his brother's speeches and notes at the JFK Presidential Library, and we were heading next to the Library of Congress to check out the rest—with Teddy's approval. Anything in there was public domain. We'd write our one man show only using Kennedy's own words. No one could stop that. They became public domain when the family donated them to the Library of Congress. Hence the title of our play, *JFK – In His Own Words*.

Fuchs was intrigued. That could work. But what about the fact that we couldn't write for HBO because they weren't signatory with the Writers Guild?

Kevin smiled at that. "Not a problem."

He went on to explain that we wouldn't be writing a TV script. That was prohibited. Instead, we'd be writing a play. And HBO had the right to buy the television rights to broadcast a produced Broadway play. Under Kevin's suggestion, HBO would commission, in advance, the cost of writing the play. We would write it. Then HBO would rent a Broadway theater for a week, mount the play and record it to which they'd own the TV rights to televise it. That simple.

And it was. We had a deal. Fuchs wondered why he hadn't figured that out before. Maybe that's because he had never met Kevin before. Two cities down; already we'd been out with a senator and sold a Broadway play. I liked this trip.

We had one more stop left in the Big Apple. Though the dreaded enemy of any Boston man was anything that had to do with the New York Yankees; that's where we were headed next. We had a meeting scheduled at Yankee Stadium with George Steinbrenner, owner of the team, and considered the Darth Vader of the Evil Empire.

We learned with mixed feelings that Mr. Steinbrenner was unavailable when we arrived. Kevin had one goal for seeing George. It was to actually bring back a souvenir for United Artists Veep Claire Townsend. She loved the Yankees and her favorite player: the great Reggie Jackson.

When Steinbrenner's assistant told us that his boss was sorry he couldn't meet with us, Kevin said there is one thing he'd like. We had schlepped that far out to Yankee Stadium from Manhattan— could we get an autographed baseball from Reggie? The assistant had surely heard that request many times before. He went to a desk, opened a drawer and pulled out an autographed ball, signed by the great slugger. They had pre-autographed baseballs from all of the team members, so this was no real chore.

We knew then that we had accomplished all that New York was going to offer up this trip. Coming home with that ball would make us heroes in Claire's eyes for sure.

So as fast as we were blowing through cities, we were adding to our arsenal of projects. We had two television pilots, a major movie studio film and now a Broadway show to write. As Kevin would beam, "the Broadway play is outside Chuck's deal too."

I wasn't sure how we were going to break that news to Chuck Fries when we returned. We still had Washington and New Orleans yet on the itinerary. I couldn't wait to see what Kevin would surprise me with in these cities.

WASHINGTON, D.C.

As the train slowly jerked forward we saw Grand Central Terminal growing smaller, then ultimately disappear behind us as we chugged on our way toward Washington, D.C. Our career was perhaps hitting the highest peak it would ever reach for us.

In the capital city, we made the obligatory visit to the ballet and actually saw a performance and afterwards met with the dancers. They were amazingly kind, friendly and truly athletic. I had no idea what it took to be a ballet performer, and ended up with the greatest appreciation for their talents and skills. It was a very hard and dedicated life. There was really no time for anything outside of the company and perhaps that's why there were so many "relationships" and ultimately feuds among many of the dancers.

The following day we visited the Library of Congress. The curator there couldn't have been any more helpful. There were volumes of books, tapes and films of President Kennedy. All of them were made available to us, courtesy of our buddy, Senator Ted, whose office took care of our arrangements. We requested certain documents be copied and sent to our office at CBS Studio Center where Chuck Fries had us housed. Regardless of how we needed to use JFK's words, we had been given permission from the highest source.

After the work portion of our research visit was completed, Kevin had one more "important" stop he'd arranged—Marine Corps Base, Quantico. Now what we two pacifists were going to do there was again shrouded in Kevin secrecy.

Quantico is where the top Marines are based. Special Ops uses their facilities; even the FBI trains its special agents there. If you're a marine, Quantico is the plumb destination you want to be affiliated with. If you were stationed there, you were the cream of the crop (or your daddy was a Congressman or Senator). You had arrived.

This was an imposing place with as much, if not more security, than Camp David. Presently we were meeting with the base commander. As we were shown into the general's office by two clean cut, parade-dressed sergeants, we were offered coffee by the commanding officer. I accepted while Kevin asked for something stronger, preferably with a "proof" number attached to it. At least he showed some restraint and didn't ask for a joint.

The two officers were dispatched to bring us our drinks. They were back in no time. When I noticed there was no cream, just some powder as an additive, the general picked up on my hesitation. He asked if I'd prefer real cream. I told him I would. Without a word one marine turned to get me some. He'd have to go to another building to secure it.

Kevin barked, "Double time, marine!" Damn, if that guy didn't tear ass out of the office to retrieve it.

When I questioned Kevin, he said that Kennedy's office arranged for us to carry the rank of lieutenant colonel while on the base. When a "light colonel" says 'go,' you ran. The impressed general smiled, asking Kevin if he had served in the military. My partner proudly replied, "Merchant Marines... Only place they'd let me keep the beard." The commander chuckled. He liked that. As a civilian, I didn't get the humor. Evidently, only in the Merchant Marines can you sport facial hair, at least at that time.

The commander got right down to business. How could he and the Marines be of service to us? Kevin then revealed his plan, though a bit cryptically, even to me.

"Davis—Monthan," Kevin revealed.

"That's Air Force," the general smiled.

"We both know you have the sway, general. A word from the top bird and we're in, no limits."

"When do you want to tour?"

"We can be in Tucson in two weeks... Air force tranny from LA requested."

What fucking language were they talking? What was going on?

Kevin continued, "Request orders for both of us through the local LA AF PR office."

"Request granted. Anything else?"

"Oh, and do you think you could arrange for us to go up on a T-38 when we're there. I always wanted to know what breaking the sound barrier feels like."

The commander started taking down notes. "Project name?"

Kevin looked at me. I had no idea what was going on, but I was starting to get cold sweats. The out-of-breath sergeant returned with two containers of cream—one regular, one half-n-half. While

I was pouring, Kevin said, "We're calling the movie *Phantom of the Boneyard*."

"Great title. Project Boneyard, for short."

"Thank you, Commander."

Within a few minutes, a military car was driving us back to The Madison, our D.C. hotel. During that ride Kevin explained what he had just done.

"We just got the Air Force, through Supreme Command, to authorize us to have free reign at the largest air force base in America—where they store all of their decommissioned planes, miles and miles of them, lined wingtip to wingtip. When they need a part, they wire D-M. D-M pulls the part from another plane and sends it off. We're going to set a movie there and get the Air Force to pay for it, trust me."

This time it wasn't "the trust" me part I was concerned with.

Kevin looked at me and said, "You gotta stop letting details get in your way. Look for the big picture."

"You must have had something in mind?"

"Yeah, yeah. It's kind of a spooky looking place. I've seen pictures. We'll do something where a pilot, shot down in Nam and presumed dead, shows up there, and locates his old plane. He secretly rebuilds it, steals some weaponry and takes to the air to shoot down his air force buddy who he thinks stole his girlfriend after he was shot down, MIA and presumed dead."

"And that's how this 'dead' guy thinks he's going to win his girlfriend back, by killing his buddy? That doesn't make any sense."

"Yeah, why not? The guy was fucked up in Nam. Just put in some big dogfight air battle at the end, good guy/bad guy shit—maybe he's even armed with a nuke that'll take out a whole city to heighten the stakes. A buddy love triangle. You're good at that crap. You'll figure it out. I just sell 'em, you write 'em."

He sure could sell them, that's for sure.

"And what's a T-38? You said something about that."

"T stands for trainer and the 38 is a fighter jet. We're going up for a ride."

"I can't. You know I'm terrified of heights."

"Don't worry. You'll probably pass out from the G-force before you get very high anyway."

He was chock full of good news. So, as fast as we were blowing through cities, we were adding to our arsenal of projects. Now, thanks to the military, we were going to probably have another movie to write. Talk about an embarrassment of riches—plays, movies, TV pilots—when were we going to breath?

And we still hadn't visited New Orleans. On the train ride from D.C. to the Crescent City, I was able to harness Kevin long enough to finish writing one of the pilots and make a good dent in the other. I also insisted that there be no more surprises in New Orleans. I had enough of them in Boston, NYC and Washington.

"Too late," he smirked, "but you'll love this one."

NEW AWLIN'S 'N HOME

When we got off "The Crescent" in the New Orleans train station, we were met by this most dignified, southern gentleman, Hank LaGrange. His family had lived in the Crescent City since the pirate days. There wasn't a Cajun jambalaya or a hurricane glass with a bourbon-based beverage in it that he didn't know about. He was aware of all of the town's skeletons. He loved nothing more than sharing those and tales of voodoo and witchcraft with two Hollywood movie types. That's why the Louisiana Film Commission had assigned him to us. He was going to be our personal guide for the three days we'd be in his exciting city.

Hank had all sorts of sights and places lined up for us to see. Bringing a movie and all the related spending to New Orleans was a big deal for the economy there. Everyone fought over getting our attention. Though I never saw it transpire, I'm sure our tour guide supplemented his own personal income with "favors" for taking us to certain locations and sites. Everywhere we went, the town's people always knew Hank. We couldn't have been treated better. He and his town car were at our disposal 24 hours a day.

Sneeze and he'd be there with a linen hanky waiting for us. Oh, how we were spoiled.

Kevin had been to New Orleans before and had told me how much I'd love it here. Aside from the French Quarter, the piping hot beignets and the Mississippi River Boat, we were going to get Hank to take us around to the best little Jazz clubs you could find anywhere. Both my wife and I loved jazz. All of these great places like Preservation Hall, Fritzels, and Sweet Lorraine's Jazz Club without her had me feeling twinges of guilt.

Our first stop was at the hotel to drop off our bags. Hank cautioned we'd have a lot to see that afternoon. He had already taken care of the check-in, handed us the keys and said we'd just have time to go freshen up. He'd see to the bags.

When I opened the door to my suite, I was a bit confused. I saw luggage there in the room on the unpacking stands already. How did Hank get that done so fast? The answer was simple. Those weren't my bags. But I wasn't in the wrong room. I had a roommate.

Suddenly my wife, who Kevin had arranged to fly out, appeared from the bathroom. This was the surprise that Kevin had alluded to. He had arranged for our wives to come out from Los Angeles and be with us for the three days before we'd take that last leg of the train trip home.

The next trio of days was amazing. Kevin and his wife, me and my wife were given royal dignitary treatment. We dined in the finest restaurants. We did some amazing sightseeing to places that weren't even open to the public. We stopped by and saw the ballet company as we were obligated to. We experienced N'awlins or New Awlins the way only Kevin could have arranged—with Hank's help and know-how, of course. There was a midnight visit to a voodoo ceremony out in some Cajun bayou wetlands. We stopped by a few 100-year-old cemeteries where all the above ground crypts were slowly sinking into the ground and supposedly spirits walked freely at night. We toured old plantations which still had slave quarters. You could easily imagine the terrible life those poor souls experienced by the remnants of their existence. We even got to touch some old bandit booty that was recovered from the days of the gentleman pirate, Jean Lafitte, and other infamous scalawags. This was some amazing town.

The time passed like three moments. We regretfully boarded the train for the last leg of the journey. As tired as we were, I was going to make sure Kevin spent some time working so we'd have the second of the two pilots completed by the time we got back to Los Angeles in a few days.

It was never hard to find Kevin on the train. He had some of his travel money that he hadn't yet spent, so he lavished it on drinks in the club car for anyone old enough to imbibe. When he got to the point that I felt he was headed for a crash, I'd round him up, see that his tab was paid and we'd go to my cabin which was set up for us to write. I had my Smith Corona portable and a ream of paper. When Kevin was loose, I only had to get him primed like a water pump and the gold nuggets of comedy flowed. He had managed to score some weed from the Skycaps. He was never at a loss for that. I'd set up what the next script scene was to be about. My partner would lie down, close his eyes, and regale me with gems faster than I could get them down.

I told him the next scene in the pilot would be at the embassy where the young leading marine would walk in on the ambassador, who was wiping tears from his eyes, very sad. Kevin asked why he was so sad. I told him we'd have to figure that out. Kevin nodded, "Let's start the scene before the marine arrives and sees the ambassador is deep in thought."

"Okay, what do you have in mind," I asked.

"The ambassador's wife enters and finds her husband sitting at his office desk. She watches as he takes a sip of fine wine and sighs. 'What's the matter, dear?' she whispers as she steps into the room."

I was taking this all down as Kevin continued. "The ambassador looks up from his wine glass. 'Just a simple case of melancholia, my dear. Do you remember back, 20 years ago, when we were dating and you were only 16?' he asks solemnly. 'Yes I do,' she replies. The ambassador pauses, then inquires, 'And do you remember when your father caught us in the back seat of my car?'"

"'How could I forget?' his wife responds. Her husband sniffles for a beat, then asks, 'Then you must remember when he shoved the shotgun in my face told me, either you marry my daughter, or I'll send you to jail for 20 years.' She chuckles slightly, 'Yes, I remember that too. Is that why you're crying?'"

"He wipes another tear from his cheek and says, 'No. It's just that would he have gotten out today.'"

With that, Kevin gently drifted off, the joint dropping on the floor, burning a small spot in the carpet. An hour or so later I woke him up and read what I had fashioned out of his cacophonous jabber during his periodic moments of waking. It turned out to be the completed second act. Interpretation was my skill, my contribution to the team and I turned out to be quite good at it. That's how Kevin and I wrote best. Give me something to work with and let me run to the finish line.

I'd read to Kevin what he "wrote" before passing out. Sometimes he'd remember it. Sometimes he wouldn't. He was continually amazed at how good it sounded after it went through my "mill" as he called it. He genuinely and respectfully called what I did writing. I called it editing...most likely the truth lies somewhere in between. In Kevin's own way, he was a man of his partner's words.

A few days later we got off the train at Los Angeles' Union Station, exhausted. We had completed both pilots. I had also written what I felt was a strong outline for the A Night at the Ballet movie. Freaking me out was knowing two new projects also needed to be tackled sooner than later—the JFK Broadway play and the movie, Phantom of the Boneyard. Overall, no trip could have been more successful.

But success had its costs. For starters, we slept most of the next two days. Then when we got back into our offices, we were met with a note "inviting" us into see Chuck. We figured he wanted to know how the trip went. Or maybe he had read the two pilots that we had messengered over to him before we went into our 48-hour hibernation. Whatever it was, we were, as the gnarly West Coast surfers would say, "riding the crest."

Turns out it was a bit of both. We reported in on the successful trip, but left off the sale of the two new projects. Kevin wanted to check with Herb, our agent, first to determine how and with whom we should proceed with those. From what Chuck was told, we'd learned a lot about the ballet which was making a good outline possible. He wanted an ETA on that to which Kevin told him, two weeks. That surprised me because I had finished it on the train, done a bang up job if I do say so myself, and didn't think Kevin would need that long to put his imprint on it.

Then Chuck buzzed into the office Malcolm Stewart, his VP of Development, who was with us when we sold both of the TV pilots. I could tell something was afoot because Mal was totally afraid of Kevin (and in turn, me—guilt by association); yet he was walking in with too much confidence, almost a swagger.

Kevin picked up on it too. He looked over to Chuck. "You know a bus station is where a bus stops. A train station is where a train stops. When Malcolm arrives, we have a work station."

That was just water off Malcolm's back. With a nod from Chuck, he revealed, "I've read your two pilot scripts."

"So," Kevin perked up, "Ready to start casting?"

"Hardly." Malcolm wasted few words.

Kevin smiled, "Then I take it you didn't like them?"

Malcolm revealed he expected, "More."

"Any more and it would be a two-parter," said Kevin. "There are more jokes in there than you'll find in a whole season of *Three's Company, Taxi* and *The Jeffersons* combined."

"Then you've hidden them well," the Veep spoke up. This wasn't like him. He was savoring this too much. "I suggest you take my scripts with my notes and consider some substantial changes."

This got Kevin going. "Good idea. I'll follow them right up your ass where I'm going to shove them. Who the fuck do you think you are? You wouldn't recognize a joke if it looked like your mother— and that would be some joke. No wonder you're an orphan. Who'd have knowingly claimed you?"

In no time this escalated into a full blown war. Kevin shot a stare over to a stunned Chuck and said, "You know, Chuck. I like you. I've sometimes taken you for granted or even for a fool. By keeping this piece of shit on your payroll you've proved the fool part." Then he turned directly on Malcolm. "Sadly, Malcolm, light travels faster than sound. That's why people, like you, appear bright until they hear you speak."

"Enough!" Chuck barked. Kevin had the boss boxed in. Who was he going to placate, his executive vice president of over 10 years or his top producer who is selling shows left and right, TV shows and movies that could make him millions. I didn't open my mouth. I didn't have to. My jaw had dropped when Kevin began his tirade.

"Look," Fries began, "I'm sure it's not that bad, either of the scripts. Just look at Malcolm's notes. Maybe there's something he sees that you didn't think of."

Kevin nodded and told Chuck that he's right. Maybe in the few weeks we've been away Malcolm discovered he's suddenly a comedy maven. Maybe he's been talking to Mel Brooks and Woody Allen and they've taught him everything they know. Staring straight at Malcolm but addressing the boss, "Chuck, just because you're a charitable Catholic and wish to hire the handicapped, that's your business. When it comes to our business, this imbecile is persona non grata. I've seen you out with your wife. You certainly know how that feels."

With that proclamation, Kevin and I got up and started to leave. "Hey, Bossman, can you have your boy here, Malcolm, send down some boxes. We quit." Then he exited. I followed. Stunned.

I just crashed down on the sofa in our office. With no consultation, no discussion, Kevin just handed in our resignation. I could tell that he didn't seem the least bit concerned. Deftly reading my facial expression—one of confusion and pain; confidently he consoled me with a simple, "Relax. I know what I'm doing."

As if reading my mind Kevin added, "Just wait. You'll see. You've got to learn to understand people like Chuck. They will always choose money over personnel. We represent money."

There came a knock on the door and Chuck entered. Played just as Kevin had expected. Chuck said he wanted to make peace. He had obligations to both us and Malcolm. Kevin couldn't help himself. "C'mon, admit it, Chuck. If brains were lard, Malcolm couldn't grease a hot frying pan."

The agreement that Chuck proposed is that he would send the pilots over as written, no changes. We'd allow Malcolm to attend the meeting at CBS in case they had any notes. Kevin said we appreciated his interceding, or actually I think he said, "coming to your senses." We would get back to him with our decision that afternoon. Kevin loved to make people wait, squirm if possible. As Chuck was leaving, Kevin called after him, "In the meantime, still have the boxes sent in case we elect to leave."

We went to lunch after Chuck's visit. We agreed to his terms and the pilots were sent over as written by us. No changes. Now we had to wait.

DID SOMEONE SAY FELLINI?

Hair extensions. Today all women wear them. They're part of most visits to a beauty shop. Well, here in my office, taped to the small wall mirror I have two payot or long, curly Jewish sideburns—ethnic hair extensions. Not exactly something I'm ever going to need again, but they do vividly bring back the reason I have them. Should I finally part with them, put them in the trash pile, which was still mostly devoid of my junk, or should I hold onto them? Sentimental value is tough to put a price on. Tossing these away isn't just getting rid of an old Halloween costume. It's giving up a touchstone that evokes a bejeweled memory from my memory's treasure chest of Kevin adventures.

*****

To pass the time while we waited for CBS to read our two pilots, Kevin thought we should drop by United Artists to bring Claire the story outline for our Marx Brothers movie and the autographed Reggie Jackson baseball. I liked the idea of getting the treatment over to her, though Kevin had never so much as said a word to me as to whether or not he liked it—or if he had read it. He blindly trusted me on things like that. He was always onto the next project or stage of one. If they liked the outline, we'd get notes. Then we'd knock out the script.

As we were going to L.A.'s Westside, that's where United Artists, MGM, and Fox studios were all located, Kevin thought we could make a publicity event out of the whole journey. He rented a stretch limo and decided to have us dress up in costume. With Kevin's salt and pepper hair and beard, he made a wonderful Greek Archbishop. We went to Western Costume, the famous house of movie attire, where he rented the vestments and colors, and even wore a bishop's mitre and carried a gold-crested crosier.

Having just grown a beard myself, Kevin felt I'd make a good Hassidic Rabbi. I was fitted in a white shirt, black pants, and long black robe. Topping it all off was an ornate skullcap. Together we'd go and pay a visit to some of the executives at the studios that we knew, and bless them. To commemorate the event, Kevin had champagne in the passenger section of the stretch limo we rented. While taking these executives for a short drive; we'd imbibe, entertain them for a few minutes and then return them. For a few of the special guests who Kevin felt comfortable with, he'd even offer them some grass or some coke (the powdered kind). In hours, word had spread around Hollywood about us two zany guys and our wacky stunt. As we drove around town, our agent, Herb, phoned us to say he was getting calls from network and studio executives all over asking for us to stop by their offices. They wanted to see this for themselves. That day, everyone wanted a piece of Hartigan and Garber craziness.

We started off at the long fountains in front of the Century Plaza Hotel in Century City. Kevin tipped off the press that some ecumenical event was going to take place at 1 p.m. At 1 sharp, our limo pulled up. We two "holy men" got out of the limo in full regalia. Kevin led a benediction for sensible fertility practices—he made the sign of the holy cross, lifted his crosier and began solemnly and with a very heavy Greek Accent:

"In days of old, when knights were bold and rubbers weren't invented, you pulled a sock, up over your cock and babies were prevented. In the name of the Father, the Son and the Holy Ghost, I now pronounce you, 'blessed waters.'"

And then the fountains, as if on cue, raised pressure and danced a bit before settling down. I still don't know how Kevin arranged for that to happen. He claimed it was divine intervention. Reporters and photographers looked upon us, stunned, as we got back into the limo and drove off. When the driver asked where to next, Kevin told him, "United Artists."

Sergeant Hollywood. Where else but at the MGM/UA Studios lot would there be a head security man with that name? He let us drive onto the lot. Before long, we were in the executive building on our way to Claire Townsend's office. It took her assistant a moment to recognize us in costume. Once recognition set in she told us we could wait in Claire's office. Claire was due back from lunch any minute, and the assistant knew she'd want to see us.

"She loves you guys. You always make her laugh. She's been under a lot of pressure lately. Your visit will do her good."

And so we went in. Five minutes, then ten minutes passed. Kevin and I were anxious to get going to a few other places. We considered just leaving the treatment for the movie with the assistant, but she said Claire had called and was moments away. She didn't tell Claire we were there. She thought she'd keep it a surprise.

Kevin and I took the Reggie Jackson signed baseball we got for her and started tossing it around the office. We didn't hear the door when it opened and continued to play catch. Suddenly we heard a thud and looked over. It was Claire. She had seen us and passed out. While her assistant dialed for help, we rushed to her and tried to comfort her. She awoke, looked up.

"Claire? Can you sit up? It's us. David and Kevin. Are you okay?" I asked her.

She took a moment to clear her head, and then she seemed fine. With our assistance, she stood up. We asked her what happened. She said, "I know you'll think I'm crazy, but when I walked in and saw you two, a priest and a rabbi; I thought my life had turned into a Fellini film and the two of you were Death coming to take me."

We had a bit of fun with that explanation as we handed her the Reggie Jackson signed baseball. It was as if she had been given the Holy Grail. Once she was back to normal, we also handed her the movie treatment.

*****

A Fellini film? Death coming to get her? That's movies. This is real life. She was only late 30s at the time. Yet too often life imitates art. Claire would be in her own Fellini film a few short years later, taking that final journey into eternity as Death's companion; much sooner than anyone could have anticipated. She would be gone at the very young age of 43, still missed today by anyone who had the privilege to meet, know or work with her.

WAITING FOR THE SHOE TO DROP

While we waited to hear from both CBS and United Artists, Kevin and I started culling the volumes of material for the JFK play. As that was more research at this time than anything else, Kevin took to making the arrangements for our upcoming trip with the air force to scout "The Boneyard" (the world's third largest air force) just outside of Davis-Monthan Air Force base.

The military was always something I left to Kevin. He loved it. I was a pacifist who luckily got a high draft lottery number when I was a student in my freshman year of college. The Vietnam War was well underway and I wanted no part of it. Back then, the draft was not voluntary as it is today; a lottery system was in effect. The lower the number you got in the lottery, the more likely you were to be drafted. I received number of 345. The speculation at the time was the cut-off that year would be 100. That is, anybody who had received a number under that would likely be drafted. I was safe. However, I stayed 1-A as a freshman, forgoing my student deferment. If I made it past the one year of eligibility, as I did, they'd never be able to call me. That's as close to the military as I got. That and our trip to Quantico. I have always respected the military. I just didn't feel I had what it takes to be part of it.

I had suggested that I stay in California and let Kevin take the trip alone; he'd come back with pictures while I would start crafting the JFK material. We expected to be hearing from CBS and UA soon. We'd never get this HBO/Broadway project done if we both left.

That all fell on deaf ears. Kevin insisted I join him. We'd be leaving tomorrow to Arizona for three days. We'd be flying out on AF transport from LA to Tucson and stay two nights, bivouacked on the D-M base there. I was hoping we could round trip it in a day; then Kevin mentioned something about our needing a day of training.

"Training for what?"

Kevin shot me an amazed look. "Our T-38 flight."

Oh, jeez, that. I didn't want to go up in any small fighter jet let alone take some kind of training. But as usual with Kevin, what did my thoughts matter? He was a one-man wrecking crew on a two-man team.

Our flight to Tucson was uneventful and the air force folks really looked after us very well. We were picked up at the base, driven by jeep to the barracks and told we'd be touring the Boneyard tomorrow with training and flying the following day. As it was still morning, I asked about the rest of this day. The AF press liaison, Major Sally Barnes, who flew with us from LA and took care of all of our scheduling and plans, said we were free to walk around, talk to the guys, check things out—"Oh, and make sure you pick up your 'G-suits' for your fighter flight."

I had no idea what a G-suit was. I figured it was some sort of flight suit. Kevin corrected me and said it was protective gear to go along with our flight suits. Its job: keep us from blacking out under the high G-forces we'd be experiencing. I did NOT sign up for this.

I had troubles with regular commercial flights. I said I needed to pass. Major Barnes, though she preferred we call her Sally, wouldn't let me out of it, nor would Kevin. It was ordered up by the Washington brass at Quantico, and it was going to be done.

My first impression of the Boneyard: overwhelming. with its acres and acres, as far as Kevin and I could see, of abandoned aircraft parked in perfect formation, aligned wingtip to wingtip, nose to tail. All the aircraft weather sealed and requiring little to make them airborne once again if called into service. Every type and size of plane the military has owned—from bi wing aircraft to recent but outdated jets. Small planes to huge cargo carriers and B-52 bombers. Helicraft too. Thousands of planes all stored and catalogued. If a part was needed to fix a craft in commission, they knew exactly where to find it. It was here in the middle of the raging hot desert.

One plane stood out in particular: a Lockheed C-121 Constellation with Columbine II painted on the side. It was unsealed and we were able to go aboard. What struck us most was the seating arrangement. Major Sally told us it was the very first Air Force One. It was created after two planes with the same call letters, one carrying President Eisenhower, the other one carrying commercial passengers, nearly collided over Colorado back in 1953. Since that time, they designated any plane with the president on board as Air Force One. Since the near miss happened over Colorado, First Lady Mamie Eisenhower nicknamed the plane after that state's flower. It became Ike's plane. Sally then showed us where the president and first lady used to sit. Between the president's and Mamie's seat was a "hidden compartment." Kevin asked if that's where the president kept his "red box" or top secrets. Sally confessed, "No, it's where Mamie used to hide her booze."

Seems the former first lady had a bit of a drinking problem, being sober ran a close second to her preferred state of mind.

It was very easy to see how this humongous site could make a great setting for a movie—a very eerie movie, as confirmed by the late afternoon setting sun, casting long shadows and the creaking of the old planes in the ever present wind. The narrative Kevin had proposed of a phantom of the opera-type story set here would be mind boggling. Major Sally said the AF and her office would and could provide us with all the permits and access we'd need. . Pilots, planes, it was all at our disposal. Only one obstacle stood in our way. We needed a studio or TV network to commission the script. That didn't seem to be much of a challenge to Kevin. We'd get it. This was one time I was sure he was right. On our way back to the barracks we thanked Sally for taking us out there. She said it was her pleasure and knew that tomorrow would be just as exciting. Our T-38 flight.

The training the next day was really just a bit of classroom. Then we were taken out onto the tarmac so we could get acquainted with our planes and our assigned pilots. The guys seemed nice, but you could tell they had a bit of an unbridled side to them. We were bearded Hollywood types and they were clean-cut Midwestern boys who were going to give us the ride of our lives, whether we liked it or not. It soon became not.

Captain Andrews was my pilot. Kevin was put in the hands of Captain Hale.

I was all suited up and climbed into the back seat. I put on my helmet and was in all my flight gear. Kevin was busy snapping pictures of me that I'm sure would someday be filed under "scared shitless". Captain Andrews indicated all the gauges to me, strapped me in and showed me "the stick." That's how this multi-million dollar machine is steered. There were pedals too, but I was too overwhelmed and anxious to remember much. I do recall looking over and seeing Kevin in the T-38 next to me, shooting me a "thumbs up" as he put his oxygen mask on.

Orientation wasn't nearly as frightening or intimidating as I had thought it would be. Then, I noticed what appeared like Kevin tapping his pilot on the shoulder and Captain Hale looking over at my plane and nodding. Knowing Kevin, I had the feeling something was up.

Soon I plugged my headset in and could hear my pilot over the ear-piece say, "Elbows In." He was going to be closing the glass canopy. As it slid airtight, I was a bit surprised, wondering why he'd do that if he was just going to orientate me on the plane at this time. As it closed, everything became quite. Peaceful. Then...

The roar of the jet engines starting up and the instant vibrations startled me. All of the gauges came to life. What was going on? This seemed a bit too real. Then it hit me, we were done with "orientation." This was now the real thing. This was the time. My pilot, sitting in his compartment in front of me looked over his shoulder and said for me to remember to breathe normally.

That was the worst thing he could have said short of we're going to crash. My heartbeat started racing and my breathing became very forced as I looked over to Kevin who shot me another thumbs up. Then his fighter plane started rolling forward, taxiing down the runway. No, this couldn't be. Were we really taking our flight now?!

Soon we were at the end of the runway and I saw Kevin's plane suddenly lurch forward and lift instantly into the sky at a gravity-defying, steep incline. As I processed what I was seeing, we jumped forward and suddenly a ton of bricks were pressing on my chest. My pilot said over the mic we were up and what I was experiencing was G-2 force on the takeoff. I have no idea how it would have felt without the special G-suit. Now that I was airborne, I wanted to land. Safely, but fast.

We climbed rapidly and before I knew it, we leveled off at about 25,000 feet. I was starting to get a little more comfortable. As we hit a little turbulence during the ascent, I had no place to put my hands to steady myself against the movement so they found their way to the side of my seat. There were two handles there which I grasped onto as we careened and veered around in the sky. I could hear the two pilots talking and saying something about cat and mouse. So I pressed my com button and asked my pilot what that meant. He told me to hold on and he'd show me.

"Oh, and whatever you do, don't grab onto the two handles on the side of the seat. The left one blows off the canopy and the right one ejects you" came the directive of the pilot. "And if we need to eject, you have to pull the left one first or you'll splat yourself going through the canopy."

Don't you think he could have shared this with me first?

Suddenly Kevin's plane, which was wingtip to wingtip with us, dove precipitously. We followed. My breakfast felt like it was going to come up one beat later. Kevin's jet evidently was the "mouse," we were the "cat" and we'd have to try to catch them. Kevin's jet went into all kinds of patterns and maneuvers. We dove, we climbed, we flew upside down, barrel rolled, we nearly stalled out a few times—I just wanted back on land. The pilot kept asking me how I felt and I think I was so scared I just nodded, like he was going to get something out of that. The rushing sound of the wind at hundreds of miles an hour, plus the roar of the thrust coming from the jet engines did me in. I was panicking. Then we gradually leveled out, and the pilot asked me if I was okay.

I lied. I said I was, thanked him for the thrill and asked him how much longer we would be up. He said we could go back any time I wished. I suggested this was the right time. He then floored me with, "She's all yours. Take her to…" and he gave me a heading.

"What the hell?" I garbled through my oxygen mask.

"You're buddy over there told me it was always a dream of yours to fly one of these babies. Well, today's your lucky day."

Stunned, I looked over and saw Kevin giving me the "thumbs up." That fucker! He wanted me to fly this bird and he knew how scared I'd be. Well, I was going to show him. I grabbed the stick when I saw my pilot, Hale, lift both his arms up over his head like he was in a hold-up. He was touching the canopy. I slowly drew the stick to the left and watched the gauges moving and the altimeter starting to drop a little. My pilot told me to keep her steady at this altitude but keep making the turn. "You're doing just fine."

I became so mind-boggled and fixated on what I was doing, I soon found myself dead-on the assigned heading. We were holding steady at about 15,000 feet. I couldn't tell the airspeed because I was too preoccupied to figure out which gauge told me that. I have to say it was a huge rush to be flying this bird. I was able to turn it and keep her steady. Not bad for a neurotic writer. About 15 minutes later, the pilot told me he would take it from there and he landed us.

It took me a few minutes to regain my composure. But I had done it. I not only took a flight, but I flew. I unharnessed myself as the pilot switched off a number of toggles and retracted the canopy. When I gladly stepped out and down onto the ground I was met by the base commander, the trainer from the classroom and our liaison, Major Sally. As they greeted me, the base commander surprisingly shook my hand and gave me a certificate with my name on it, certifying that I had officially logged one hour of flight time training and piloting a T-38 Jet.

The first thought that came to my mind as I looked at it was how proud my father, a private pilot in his own right, would be of me at that moment. I had just done something that he could only have dreamed of. I owed that all to Kevin.

No matter how much you could hate or despise something Kevin said or did, there was always that accompanying, redeeming moment. As Kevin made his way over to me, he was beaming from ear to ear. He knew what he was doing. He was helping me get over my fear of heights and flight, a fear that has never returned. I never could have accomplished that without Kevin. Though I think he garnered just as much pleasure from putting me through this hell as the benefits I reaped from this exhilarating experience. That was the hidden, sadistic part of this man.

STEVE BOARDNER'S

As I continued to stare at my flight certificate from my piloting the T-38, all of these memories were just reminding me of the history I had with Kevin, and that his fate was but a phone call away. I quickly realized I was tossing things away that had great meaning to me. I know it would make my wife happy to see my office finally cleared of all the "debris" as she would call it, but I had to stop and compose my thoughts. Was I now discarding things and throwing them away too easily. Maybe I'd need these things sometime down the road.

I had to slow down, take some time. With my mind so clouded, I couldn't rush this process. Word on Kevin's condition would come in due time. I hadn't even bothered to check with my doctor to see if Kevin's liver donation, in case of his demise, was even a possibility. As eager as I was to hear some good news, I'd just wait. All in good time. Truthfully, I didn't want a new liver. I just wanted my friend back.

I settled in and started rocking gently in my office chair, remembering back to asking Kevin for a hand one time when we were over-booked and I was afraid we might miss some delivery deadlines.

"Helen Waite is now in charge of all rush orders," he intoned. "If you're in a hurry, just go to Helen Waite." That's how Kevin responded to my request for a line that day when I needed one last joke for the final draft of the script for *A Night at the Ballet* which we would hand in tomorrow. I was feeling overwhelmed and he was taking it all in stride. Mr. Cool as a Cucumber.

While I was churning away, throwing some sort of final touches into the UA script, Kevin was preoccupied, busying himself with his next shiny object: preparing to toss a special birthday party for our friend, Snag. Nobody knew how old our buddy really was, but we did know that another one of his birthdays was coming up in about two weeks. Kevin wanted to do something special this year. Something not only Snag would remember, but maybe the industry would take notice of as well.

On top of his health failing due to diabetes and other age-related issues, his sight was going too. He could still see, but not very well. His coke bottle glasses barely allowed him to get about. He could no longer drive which in LA is truly a handicap. Yet despite all this, his mind was still as sharp as ever. Kevin wanted to reward that while he could still appreciate it.

"No one deserves to be discarded; especially those who've made us laugh." Kevin's focus was on correcting, if even only for a few hours, the shunning of a once great man. Kevin wasn't doing this for himself. He did plenty of self-serving things. But this was from his heart and when he tossed that into life's gumbo, you got a bowl of greatness and the unexpected.

First we had to pick a spot for the party. It had to be different. It had to be Hollywood. It had to be—Steve Boardner's—a legendary Hollywood bar. What a history to that place. Legend has it that it's the last bar where Elizabeth Short drank before she stepped into the night and became better known as the Black Dahlia. It's from that establishment that the owner bailed out acting great and longtime customer Robert Mitchum after his famous pot bust. It's the bar where it's claimed that a ghost had been seen in the tiny women's restroom, and where on Christmas night one of the owners slumped over dead while downing a double shot of Patron. Yup. This was sure the right place.

Now we needed guests. Kevin and I manned the phones, calling everyone we knew, even some we didn't. Dignitaries. Actors. Musicians. Local politicians. Military personnel. Crafts people. Writers. Directors. Studio brass. Basically if you ever worked in Hollywood, especially if you ever worked with Snag, we tracked you down and invited you. When all was said and done, we had over 100 RSVPs. Quite a turn out for this old man. Maybe it was just for the free lunch? But it didn't matter, we had guests.

We had hoped for a surprise visit from Jackie Gleason, but he bowed out, staying in Miami where he was living. He was too ill to make the trip, but promised to call or write. One nugget we did get from him was that Snag once had a writing partner, Hank, whom we didn't know existed. Through the Writers Guild, we found him. We invited Hank and arranged for him to get there early, so we could surprise Snag.

All Snag knew was Kevin and I, along with our wives, wanted to take him to lunch for his birthday. He had no idea there was going to be a party.

We picked him up and when we got to Boardner's, we told Snag that our wives were going to make sure our table was ready. Till then, we'd grab a drink at the bar. He was no stranger to bending an elbow so he said, "Yes."

No matter how solid your plans or how fine the intentions...

Snag leaned into us as the bartender deposited our drinks. He whispered, "See that guy at the end of the bar? That's my old partner, Hank."

Kevin and I feigned surprise and suggested we invite him over, talk about old times. Snag said with undeniable authority, "No. I hate that guy!"

Little did Snag know he was already invited to the party. Oh, well. We couldn't uninvite him. We would simply have to see what other surprises awaited us. Our wives came to the bar and announced that our table was ready. We all walked into the main room—that was packed with Snag's friends—to a thunderous shout of, "Surprise!!!"

Everyone in the room (we had bought out the entire restaurant) was an invited guest. Snag couldn't get over it. The guests all stood and applauded as we walked past them to a special, head table. We explained to Snag what was going on. He was stunned. One by one, people came to Snag's table to give personal tribute, both for his birthday and for his career. If Snag knew them, he greeted them. If he didn't, we introduced them. There was a military contingency led by Major Sally Barnes from the air force with whom we had gone to the Davis-Monthan Air Force Base. There were members of the Directors, Writers and Screen Actors guilds as well as the heads of IATSE, the major crafts union. All of the development executives from the studios and networks were there. Old faces. New faces.

We had arranged a special lunch and soon everyone was served. The place was somewhat of a novelty, not just because of history but because every table had a number on it and as well as an old, rotary phone. If you saw someone you knew or wanted to "pick up," you could ring them from your table phone. In the old days, the stars went to the Musso and Frank Grill on Hollywood Boulevard, and the below-the-line grunts went to Boardner's, around the corner on Cherokee Avenue.

Kevin opened the event with a short speech. He talked of Snag's early beginnings as dancer and magician in vaudeville. "He used to open his magic act with, 'For my first trick, I need a condom, and a volunteer.'" From that opening, the assembled got the idea this was going to be a comedy roast and no one did it better than Hartigan.

"From eight shows a week, he went into medicine. What a lot of you don't know is that Snag was a physician. Oh, yes. Now, I didn't say he went to medical school. He got his degree from one of those matchbook covers that read, 'Can you draw me?' He did and was certified. It's not that big a career jump as you may think. He swapped the Lowe's and Winter Garden Theater for the Cedars Sinai operating theater. Some of his earliest surgeries produced some of the most memorable medical quotes to this day:"

-"Oops! Hey, has anyone ever survived 500 ml of this stuff before?"

-"Ya' know... there's big money in kidneys... and this guy's got two of 'em."

-"Wait a minute, if this is his spleen, then what did I just remove?"

-"Oh, no! I think I lost my Rolex."

-"Sterile, schmerile. The floor's clean, right?"

-"What do you mean he wasn't in for a sex change?"

-"Better save that. We'll need it for the autopsy."

The audience needed a moment to catch their breaths, so Kevin took a sip of his scotch. Then he continued on.

"As you can see, it didn't bode for a long medical career, so that brought Snag back to the drawing board. With a name like Snag, comedy had to be his life. So he did what came naturally. He became a gigolo. And when that didn't work, a writer. Hey, prostitution is prostitution. Snag, the man, was armed with two indispensable bits of philosophy. First, 'dyslexics have more nuf'... and 'Kinky is using a feather, perverted is using the whole chicken.' And so his long and illustrious career took off. At this time, I want to show you some kinescopes of some of Snag's earliest work."

The lights were dimmed and Kevin put on the projector. As it started to flicker with moving images, Kevin stood by Snag, arm around him on one side, and me on the other side. The old showman offered up a little explanation or introduction for each clip, as they revealed an array of historical moments, displaying the "greats" that Snag had worked for.

As each clip played, Snag narrated. "That guy there's Durante, better known as 'the Schnoz.'" "That little cutie is Judy Garland. It was her birthday party." "Oh, that's Martin and Lewis in Vegas horsing around Sinatra's pool."

Then Kevin had snuck in a porno clip of a woman giving her well-endowed costar fellatio. Snag just stared a moment, rubbed his eyes, then slyly added, "That one there's some actress believing me when I said no starlet ever went wrong in this industry blowing the writer."

He was quick. When the clips were over, everyone applauded and you could tell this was among the proudest moments in his life. It was five minutes of the greatest names ever from stage, screen or

TV. Snag knew them all. Many of the invited guests didn't have any idea who some of these luminaries were, but it didn't matter. In their day and in Snag's, they were all somebodies. And Kevin gave them life once again, as he had done with our aging writer friend. Today, Snag was a somebody.

As people settled back into their seats, Kevin introduced a Los Angeles City Councilman. Kevin and I had arranged for this day to be officially proclaimed Snag Werris Day. Along with the councilman's gracious speech came a beautiful, decorative commemoration—a scroll that had many official "Whereas" and "Therefores" ornately scrawled, as well as the official seal of the City of Los Angeles, the mayor's signature, and the names of the full city council.

Next Kevin read aloud a few congratulatory letters and telegrams that had been sent from those people Kevin could contact. They were from the likes of Jackie —Gleason—or "John" as Snag called him—who sent along his best wishes. Then there was the telegram from the families of Bud Abbott and Lou Costello, thanking Snag for writing two of their dads' favorite movies. And finally there was a telegram from Mae West. Snag was surprised by that one. He had never worked with her. Kevin mused, "Maybe she worked on you. Where do you think that blow job clip came from?"

"Now I remember," retorted Snag. "Did you know she was really a man?" He brought down the house.

"Finally, Snag, this celebration wouldn't be complete without special closing kudos." Kevin motioned for me to bring in our last surprise. "In Hollywood, all of the greats have a star on the walk of fame. And today, in your honor, we've arranged for you to get yours."

As I wheeled in a gurney sized, draped dolly, there was an audible murmur going through the crowd. Kevin continued, "As you know, for each honoree, an appropriate symbol is placed in the center of the star—a microphone for a radio personality, a TV for a television star, a movie projector for a film personality. So in your honor and adorned with what you're best known for, here is your star.

With that Snag removed the cloth cover and there it was. A perfect cake replica of a star from the Hollywood Walk of Fame, only in the center, where the symbol goes, was an erect penis – maybe 15 inches high. Kevin graced it with, "To the biggest cocksucker in Hollywood."

Everyone broke into laughter—but Snag, through the haze of his poor vision, took a moment before it all registered. Then, with steely voice and perfect timing he added, "What? Couldn't they make one life size?"

As applause broke out for this most deserving man, Kevin genuinely embraced him. For a fellow that rarely showed emotion in public, tears dripped down the Irishman's cheeks. We had given our friend a day he'd talk about for the rest of his life.

THE VERDICT IS IN

Back at CFP, we had gotten a call from Andy Siegel, CBS's Vice President of Comedy Development. The network people had read both of our pilots and were ready for us to come in and discuss them. We had agreed that Malcolm would accompany us, so true to our word, we called and told him about the meeting. He said he'd be there.

Those people, who thrive on adrenaline, live for days like this. Not unlike the moments before your teacher would hand out your graded mid-term exam papers, we were heading for a verdict. Soon we'd know what the ultimate buyer for our shows would think of our efforts. If that pressure wasn't enough, we had Malcolm with us. Despite being on our team, we knew Malcolm secretly hoped we'd fall flat on our faces. This would justify him in Chuck Fries' eyes.

Malcolm carried his marked up copies of both our scripts, as if to demonstrate to the world his rebuke of our words. We knew this because normally, he'd have any script he'd bring to a meeting in his briefcase. The customary practice in the industry among those who read and give notes on scripts is to jot down notes and comments on a page, then dog-ear the page so those notes could be quickly found. Generally a well-received script had few downturned page corners. Scripts with problems had nearly every page dog-eared. You didn't have to look at a script for more than a second when you walked in to know if you were in trouble or not. Malcolm intentionally brought his "troubled" scripts along. Usually an executive, along with the writers getting the notes, came in with clean copies so they could start from scratch. Mal was making his statement, and Kevin took notice.

"Hey, Mr. Charm," Kevin nudged Mal. "I see you brought your scripts. Hope you didn't get any paper cuts dog-earing all those pages."

Malcolm wasn't going to be agitated over this. He kept his cool. He was going to make his stand in Andy Siegel's office where it would really register. So Kevin decided to wear him down a bit. He knew what he was doing. He had a plan. "You know, Malcolm, I don't disrespect you for having a difference of opinion. It's just that if I was to agree with you, we'd both be wrong. David knocked out two great scripts here."

What? Suddenly the blame or credit was all headed my way.

The Fries' executive just looked over to Kevin and muttered, "All I asked for was a strong script and I got this."

That didn't faze Kevin. "Let me tell you a little story, Mal. When I was a kid, I asked God before Christmas to give me a bike. But I knew God didn't work that way. So you know what I did? I stole a bike. Right out of my neighbor's garage. Christmas Day I prayed to Him for forgiveness. That I knew he gave—and you know what? I got the bike *and* forgiveness. Unless you think I'm God, don't expect the same from me."

Andy arrived with all smiles and told us to come in. As we followed into his office, Kevin sidled up to Malcolm and quietly warned, "The last thing I want to do is hurt you. But it's still on the list."

As soon as we sat down, Andy inquired how we were doing. Kevin replied, "Better today."

The vice president was a bit taken aback. "What happened?"

Kevin began, as only this bold Irishman could. "The other night I tied one on pretty good. I left the bar, more than just a bit tipsy, with just my car key in my hand. As I'm looking around to see where I left my car, this cop comes up to me and asks, 'Can I help you, sir.' I kind of stumbled back and it was quite evident I was drunk. 'Yes! Somebody stole my car,' I told him. Then he asked me, 'Where was it the last time you saw it?' So I told him, 'Last I remember, it was on the end of my key.' I guess it was about this time that the police officer noticed my fly was open and my 'you know what' was hanging out. The cop says to me, 'Sir are you aware that you are exposing yourself?' I looked down, and blurted out, 'Holy shit! My girlfriend's gone, too!'"

Andy was a sucker for Kevin's tales and even dour Malcolm couldn't help but smile at that one.

"So," Andy said, "let's get into your scripts, shall we? The first one, *Local 141*, I think shows a lot of promise. I like the story, the characters pop and there's some fun jokes in there. I'll get to that in a second... But the first one, *The Thin Blue Line*, is a bit troublesome."

Oh, the smile that took over Malcolm's face was like the Grand Canyon. He jumped in with both feet. "I had concerns, too. It was missing the essential story elements, I thought the characters were a bit underdeveloped and truthfully I didn't get the humor."

Andy said he wouldn't go that far.

Kevin, indicating the Fries Company executive added, "I think someone OD'd on his Ritalin this morning."

Andy wasn't sure how to respond to that. And he didn't have to. Kevin wasn't done yet. He addressed Malcolm, "You know what they do with foreskins after circumcision? They plant them and they grow up to become Fries Company VPs."

Andy picked up his plentifully, dog-eared pages script. He started on page one and after a few notes, we noticed a pattern here. Impatient, Kevin spoke up. "So what you're saying is you don't think it's very funny. Is that a fair assessment?"

Andy reluctantly nodded. "You know, when you guys came in and pitched this to me, I was roaring. I thought it was the funniest idea. Your characters came alive, the jokes were flowing—it had life, vigor. That's why I bought it."

I told Andy I was sorry he felt that way. We actually think it's pretty funny. That's when our CFP representative tossed in his two cents worth. "I tried to tell them, but they wouldn't listen."

Kevin turned to the CBS exec and went on the defense. "You know, Andy, humor is in the eye of the beholder, except in Malcolm's case blindness runs in his family. Think of it this way— are dolphins so smart that they can train people to stand on the very edge of the pool and throw them fish?"

I added, "Or are they trained to come up for the food when they see the trainer standing on the edge?"

"It's all your perspective, or your point of view." Kevin buttoned the thought. "And maybe we can help you and…" he looked over to the stunned Malcolm, then back to the CBS exec and continued on, ignoring the CFP veep, "… let us demonstrate so you'll understand our take. Pick a number, one to 42."

"You going to do a magic trick?" Andy queried. "We really should stick with my notes on this script."

I told him we will. "It's a 42 page script. Just pick a number." Andy chose 18.

Kevin asked everyone to turn to page 18. To Malcolm he said, "That's a two digit number with a one and an eight, in that order."

While Malcolm snarled, Kevin and I started to read it, just as written, but with us playing the characters. Three big laughs on the page from Andy. Kevin then asked for another number. Andy indicated 25. We repeated the process and had Andy laughing out loud two more times with our delivery.

"See," Kevin said. "It's perspective."

Andy complimented us and said that it was us. We were what made it funny. We told him it would be funnier yet with professional comic actors.

Now the CBS veep was convinced. We said we'd take whatever notes he wanted, but he said, "No. You've sold me. And forget the notes on the other script. Let me talk it over internally. We'll get back to you soon."

Kevin had pulled it off. Or maybe we had. I'm not sure Kevin even knew what was on each script page. It was all fashioned out of his scraps of material, which I had sewn into a very workable quilt.

That afternoon we received two memorable phone calls. The first was from Claire Townsend over at United Artists. She set up a meeting for us the next morning. She had read the full story treatment and wanted to talk it over along with some other execs from the studio. We perceived from the conversation that she liked it.

The second call was from Andy. They had gone into committee on *The Thin Blue Line* script, the one about marines on embassy duty in South America. Based on our meeting that day, the CBS network was ordering up a pilot to be shot. We got the green light. We had permission to go out, start casting and putting together a show. They'd have to work out the budget matters with the Fries Company, but we were a "go."

We went in to tell Chuck and truthfully, he was most gracious. He wanted to buzz Malcolm so he could come in and get the good news directly from Kevin. When he arrived, Kevin had already heard from CBS.

We also shared that we were going into UA tomorrow to get notes on A *Night at the Ballet*. Chuck confessed he hadn't read the 25 page treatment but Malcolm had. Surprisingly, Kevin asked Malcolm to come along with us. We already knew that the studio was predisposed to like it, so there didn't seem any harm in bringing Mal. Maybe it would even warm the waters between him and Kevin.

Without any prodding, Malcolm said he'd be glad to go and that he thought the story for that project was actually quite funny and very Marx Brothers. Of course he was old enough to get that quartet's humor. On one hand it was a huge compliment and on the other, quite reassuring that he wasn't coming along to try and sabotage us. Kevin, playfully this time, smiled at Chuck and said he'd be pleased to have a progressive thinker like Malcolm along with us. "After all, isn't he the one who said of color TV, I won't believe it until I see it in black and white?"

Chuck shook his head and told us to get out. He had work to do.

"I'm starting a new movie of the week tomorrow."

Kevin and I headed for the door on that until my partner stopped and quizzically looked back at the boss, "Makes you wonder, doesn't it. Why should people go out and pay to see bad movies when they can stay home and see one of yours on TV for nothing?"

On that we left.

Claire met us with her warm smile as we entered her office the next day at UA. Standing alongside her were two studio executives, junior to her but in the development division none-the-less. We saw they had their copies of the outline in their hands. Claire's copy was on her desk, next to the Reggie Jackson autographed baseball which she thanked us for again. As we all sat, Claire grabbed her copy of the treatment. Both Kevin and I noticed there were only two dog-eared pages, so we felt pretty confident.

It wouldn't be an official meeting if Kevin didn't have something smart to say to kick things off. "Before we start, Claire, I want to tell you that I'm a good Catholic. Before coming in here, not knowing what to expect, I went to church. I lit candles, said rosaries, and partook of the holy sacrament. David and Malcolm on the other hand both went to temple... but I had to explain to them going to temple doesn't make you any more of a Jew than standing in a garage makes you a car."

The UA execs all found it amusing which motivated Kevin to finish it off with—"And we all know that if they were true Jews, they'd have a two picture deal at Metro."

Kevin, on the heels of yesterday's pick-up of our pilot and the indication earlier from Claire that *A Night at the Ballet* was in good shape, was a bit happy-go-lucky. I knew him well enough to sense this. Until someone actually told him to stop, he'd continue on—and he did. He loved to entertain.

Then something quite unusual happened. Malcolm, who for the most part could have been played by Claude Raines as the invisible man, spoke up. "Before we get started with notes, I wanted to share some good news with you... Yesterday, CBS ordered into production a pilot Kevin and David wrote."

Everyone seemed impressed and maybe that even boosted our stock a little with UA. What a surprise that Malcolm would open up this way. It was nice and certainly not what we would have expected. You couldn't help but wonder if he didn't he have something up his sleeve?

"Okay, Kevin, let's get to the notes," I moved us all along.

Claire started off. We all read it. "It's very good and it's very funny," she said. Then there was an odd, strained pause.

"But?" I broke the silence.

"It's, how do I put this, the same story as the one you pitched me. The one I bought." Her response, as usual, was concise.

Kevin figured that was a good thing. "What did you expect? That's what you paid us to do."

She unpredictably started to get a little testy. Claire didn't hide her attitude very well. "Give me that attitude shit and the picture's dead, got it?"

Whoa. Where was that coming from?

Malcolm jumped in. "What I'm hearing is: though you liked what the boys wrote, and it was the story they sold you, you didn't see any changes to the characters from their pitch to their treatment. There were no surprises."

"Exactly," she nodded. "I wanted to see more. So my notes are simple. Give me more of the same funny stuff. And a few surprises. Should be easy enough."

It's funny how people who don't write think making changes is simple. You just sit down and add a couple of things and it's all fixed. They don't take into consideration that everything is tied into everything else. Jokes take setting up. They're not just punchlines. If you change one thing here, it impacts something elsewhere in the story. Message received. Kevin and I got it.

Claire looked over to the other UA executives. "Anyone else have anything to add?" There were just shakes of the head. Claire rose to her feet, followed by all of us and she bid us adieu. Upon leaving she assured us this was the funniest movie treatment she'd ever read.

Yeah, we thought, so why are we going away to fix it? Our five minute meeting, including four minutes of Kevin riffing, was over.

It was at this point that we looked at her differently for the first time. She went from being a charming studio executive to being a hard-nosed, defiant diplomat; essentially telling us to go to hell but in such a way that you will look forward to the trip. She was Hollywood, or so we were learning.

For the first time, we saw what value Malcolm served, mediator. Perhaps that's why Chuck kept him on. Maybe he wasn't such a bad guy after all. Now what we had to do is go back to the studio and make something good, gooder—be different, but the same. Should be easy enough, at least according to Claire.

THE HONEYMOONER'S OVER

The headline of the LA Times on January 22, 1981, read, "444 Days and Over." Now here's a yellowed, slightly torn newspaper that I had been holding onto for over 30 years. It had one meaning to the world. It had a totally different one to me and Kevin. I would gladly have put this fourth estate journal in the toss/junk pile. I pondered how prescient it was and how meaningful it would be to our future. Which pile to put this in? It wouldn't be an easy choice.

Four hundred and forty four days. That was the length of the Iran hostage crisis that began in 1979 and ended in early, 1981. To those brave souls who endured, there were multiples of others also affected by this tragedy. Fortunately, it ended well for most of them. Not so for us.

The illegal arms for hostages and the Iran-Contra scandal by President Reagan may have saved lives and families; for that gratitude seems warranted. He, like Kevin, believed that the ends justify the means. For our career, these events extracted a price. A "perfect storm" was impending.

CBS had green lit the pilot of our show, *The Thin Blue Line*, a comedy about marines on embassy duty. With this embassy raid in Iran, there was no way the public was in any mood for laughs in that arena so the network kept holding off on giving us a production start date. All we had were prayers and hopes for the victims. The overthrow lasted so long, it festered extremist fears which is generally not fodder for humor. So the network ultimately reacted as could be expected.

We got a call from Andy Siegel at the Eye Network and he passed along the word that they were going to drop *The Thin Blue Line* from their development slate. He felt badly as they had made a commitment to us but under the circumstances, they couldn't go ahead. We easily understood. There were no hard feelings toward that decision. It was the right thing to do.

What surprised us was that the network decided to make up for the cancellation by giving us a blind pilot deal. To replace the show that we lost, they'd give us another one. All we had to do is come up with an idea.

Fortunately for us coming up with ideas was an easy thing to do. Within hours, we had the show. It started with Kevin and me taking a drive over to see our old friend Snag. He was always good for a joke or two, something to cheer you up. We told him about the actions of the network, and he told us some stories about his early days in show business. He always began with, "Back in my day." Then he'd tell some delicious tale about a famous star or film or scandal. He had a million stories and loved nothing more than sharing them.

I remember saying to Snag, "Looking back, what would you say was the funniest gag you ever wrote," or "Looking back, who was the biggest bastard you ever worked with?" Kevin and I would then listen intently as we'd be regaled with legendary yarns. Then I asked Snag, "Lookin' back…"

Kevin stopped me right there. "Lookin' Back. That's our blind commitment to the network. We'll do a comedy variety show with each episode looking back at a week in time—entertainment, news, fashion, automobiles, scandals, products, commercials— you name it and we'd cover it with lighthearted reminiscences and a comedy sketch or two.

I loved the idea. So did Snag. He even offered his collection of kinescopes from the Dumont Network (1946-1956). In that collection were the eight original "Honeymooners" episodes with Jackie Gleason and Pert Kelton as his wife (later played by Audrey Meadows.) Art Carney was in them too, but he played a cop, not a garbage man or sanitation engineer as he would put it. These shows were priceless as they were the only recorded copies in existence.

Kevin said that we'd use all of that—even the old commercials which were on these reels. In their time, the shows were broadcast live. Kinescopes were 16mm films of a television broadcast, filmed off a TV as the show was broadcast to the East Coast. These films were quickly developed and flown to Chicago and Los Angeles. There was no transcontinental television broadcast mechanism or hookup for the country to see the same show simultaneously across the US. So, Chicago was the broadcast hub for the Mid-western states broadcast—and Los Angeles for West Coast viewing.

There also was no such thing as reruns in the late '40s and early '50s. After the show would air, the two copies would be sent back to the network in New York and because of the war effort, the metal reels were kept. The film was burned. History disappeared. Fortunately, Snag had salvaged a number of these —shows—the ones he wrote for, like *Cavalcade of Stars,* and held onto them. In many instances these shows were hysterical. They were filmed live and included all the flubs and mistakes and pauses for forgotten lines, missed lyrics or some actor breaking up when a piece of scenery would fall over. It was live TV; there were no second takes.

We contacted CBS with the concept and they flipped for it. Safe. No controversy and cheap to produce. Kevin and I suggested one weekly segment called Snag's Corner where we would pick up Snag on stage in his "viewing room." He'd regale us with one of his great stories, and we'd show some archival footage. The network brass loved it. The rest of the show would be pulled together from whatever resources we could. We'd bring on stars and celebs from those old days—whatever week we were featuring. We'd celebrate with sketches, song and production numbers. For variety, we'd feature an occasional fashion show or a parade of new model cars from that episode's featured week.

The reaction to the concept was so strong that we were rushed into production on the pilot. They wanted this show immediately. Here we had lost a sitcom pilot but picked up something with just as much heat.

With only four weeks to deliver *Lookin' Back* we were under the gun and had to start writing. For the pilot, we arbitrarily chose a date in mid-February, 1962. We had to really jump on the writing; so Kevin and I took our normal positions. Kevin reclined and posited, "That's the week Jackie Kennedy gave Charles Collingwood and the world a televised tour of the White House. Let's do a send up of that as our cold opening. Jackie leads Collingwood and the camera crew into the Oval Office where she's surprised to find her husband working away.

Kevin took on all the speaking roles. "Oh, Jack, I'm so sorry. I didn't know you were still working here. We'll come back later," the first lady would offer.

"Nonsense, Jackie," Kevin replied doing his excellent JFK impression. "Welcome, America. Come right in. Just signing a few checks."

Then Jackie interjects, "Don't you mean signing a few bills?"

"I wish. No. These are checks. Daddy's making me pay for those extra votes he bought me in Chicago. Then I'm off to play hide 'n' seek."

Mrs. Kennedy looks to Collingwood. "The President is such a good father. He always makes time for the kids."

JFK corrects her. "This time it's with Lyndon. He wants me to sign some crazy oil drilling rights bill. I've got to hide before I lose the entire Southern vote in the next election."

Mrs. Kennedy laughs as Collingwood looks to JFK. "Mr. President, perhaps the viewers at home would like to know about your proudest moment thus far as President."

"Actually, Mr. Collingwood, I'd say my proudest moment was before all of this. It was when I, eh, married, Jacqueline."

She reacts, "Isn't he sweet? *Je t'aime aussi.*"

"I'm reminded of our honeymoon in the Lesser Antilles. My father bought them for us as a wedding gift."

Jack looks into the camera, "I remember taking my beautiful, blushing bride in my reassuring arms while I offered her my honor. And she enthusiastically, I must confess, honored my offer.

And that's the way it went for the better part of a fortnight between us – offer and honor, honor and offer."

We finished the tour of the White House in script just as the doorbell rang. Things would start for real once the two people we were waiting for arrived.

Our new assistant, Tom Palmer was the first to appear. He was part of the internship program from the Academy of Television Arts and Sciences—the people who give out the Emmys. He had never worked a day in the industry, but I picked him out from a number of amazingly qualified candidates whom we interviewed. He was young, had a subtle sense of humor, but most of all, he was charming. And having Kevin as part of any equation meant we could never have enough charm for adequate counter-balance.

The choice of intern was left to me. Three reasons: First, I was a member of the TV Academy writers' branch. Second, I have some decent people assessment skills. And third, and perhaps most telling, on that day of the interviews Kevin was so piss drunk that he was totally M.I.A.

So when Tom showed up, I introduced him to Kevin. Now, I had prepared Tom by telling him that he was stepping into a unique situation and warned him to be ready for anything.

"Tom, this is my partner, Kevin Hartigan. Kevin, this is Tom Palmer, our new intern."

Years later, that would be recognized as the meeting of two enormous talents who during their reign would be responsible for creative greatness. Tom would go on to become executive producer and run TV's number one comedy hit, *Murphy Brown* with Candice Bergin and later work as a producer on the popular and greatly lauded, *Mad Men*.

Kevin immediately got down to business. He lit up a joint, took a deep hit, and held out the spliff to the newest member of our team. Tom passed on the opportunity, not so much because he was a goody-two shoe, but because he was more stunned than anything else.

Kevin shrugged, took back the blunt and queried Tom, "Coke?"

He wasn't talking about the beverage either when he pulled out an amber, one-gram vial accompanied by a tiny, sterling-silver spoon. Tom waved that off as well.

This too familiar opening salvo was interrupted by a knock at the door. Kevin moved to open it as a mortified Tom used a nearby newspaper to cover the ashtray which held the joint and the vial of cocaine. He used another section of the Los Angeles Times to fan the air, hoping to dissipate the waft of thick smoke still looming over the coffee table in Kevin's expansive Hancock Park living room.

When the door opened, standing there was Snag. Kevin escorted him in and sat him down with Tom.

"Who's the kid and what's he gonna cost me?" Snag asked while sizing up our intern.

Kevin introduced them and assured Snag, "The kid isn't going to cost you anything."

"Good, cuz he looks like he's worth at least two bits and I don't carry that kind of cash on me."

Kevin gave Tom a little taste of Snag's background. "Tom, this man has worked with everybody in show business. You are sitting in the shadow of greatness."

Snag puffed his chest, "Astaire and Grant, now they were greatness. I'm just the essence that made them great."

"There's yet to be a celebrity worth anything in this town who Snag hasn't worked with. Go ahead, toss him any name," Kevin challenged. "Even the old timers. Groucho. Gable. Hepburn. He knew them all."

Tom didn't know exactly what to make of this dare, so he paused, trying to come up with a name. Finally, he nervously shrugged and inquired, "Have you ever worked with Oscar winner, Broderick Crawford?"

"No!" came the instant reply.

Snag glared at Tom. Then emphatically he waited a meaningful beat before adding, "But I did work with his mother Helen in vaudeville, and was she a c*nt."

Perfect timing. That was Snag.

We flew through the next two weeks with Tom and Snag taking care of "Snag's Corner" which was going to be the centerpiece for our show. We had hired a very fine variety director and were set with our supporting cast. Now all we needed was to move to our sound stage and begin rehearsals.

Everybody seemed happy and there was even a bit of buzz beginning to flow in town about our show. Word was "accidentally" slipped out through Kevin that we would be showing the kinescope of the very first *The Honeymooners* to ever air in 1949, replete with an introduction by Jackie Gleason. My partner was never one to keep the lid on anything he was involved with. As they said in World War II, "Loose lips sink ships."

Everything sailed along as we got into rehearsals. That's when the shit hit the fan. Suddenly legal affairs at the studio contacted us. We were denied "Errors and Omissions" insurance. E & O as it's known in the industry is the coverage all programs have so that if someone sues a show over anything, slander, copyright infringement, other proprietary interests the network and studios were indemnified.

It seems that the guilds were looking for money for the actors, the writers and the directors for the kinescope segments. Even though the contracts the artists signed in those early days didn't provide for any payments for reuse, the guilds were making demands...and loudly. This was, in Kevin's eyes, purely screaming over spilled milk. There was no such thing as reruns or reuse when the contracts were signed. Using that logic, the guilds fired an opening salvo claiming we had no right to rebroadcast those kinescopes, period. From there, the guilds backed down a bit, asking for some lump sum fees to be given to each one of their general retirement funds. Kevin felt the people who actually worked on these old shows were due something, but not the kind of contributions the guilds were asking.

The more the fight went on, the more difficult it became. Then the crafts unions heard about it and wanted a taste added to their pension fund. Kevin took the position that if we paid in any money, these remunerations should go to the actual participants (or if deceased, to their family), not a general fund. Most of the performers, writers and crew were still alive. They should get the reuse pay. The guilds thought differently. They didn't want to start a precedent should other footage surface someday. They wanted the general fund to be the recipient giving the various guilds control over how the money was disbursed.

Toss in a few lawyers for good luck and you had a real donnybrook. And when no cooler minds could settle on any of this, the network, seemingly so benevolent when handing out the make-good on our pilot, called a time out and dropped the show. They didn't want to stand up to the unions.

There we were. Kevin and I went from a solid sitcom script, *The Thin Blue Line*, to an international uprising, a presidential scandal, then to a replacement show, *Lookin' Back*, to finally nothing. All we did was work our asses off. It was a foreshadowing of things to come, a change in wind direction and the beginning of some very choppy seas ahead.

COKE WITH THAT PIZZA?

The front page of Variety, The Hollywood Reporter and the Los Angeles Times all carried the same headline that Monday morning.

Hollywood Writer Dead

Hollywood writer/producer Kevin Hartigan, 39, was found this morning in McArthur Park, Hollywood Park, and the Disneyland Amusement Park in what police are calling a brutal mob hit. "It was a message," said the Chief. "Pieces of the deceased were found everywhere. We're still looking for his spleen."

That, at least, is how Kevin described his predicament. Crisis is more like it. There's reason they came up with that word. This would be one of those times. There was true panic in his voice when he called me Sunday night at 2 a.m. just days after the network had killed Lookin' Back. He was in trouble, again. *Big* trouble this time.

Kevin, like much of Hollywood in the early '80s, had an obsession with recreational drug usage—marijuana and cocaine. Now the "grass" wasn't too much of a problem, but facts are facts—if you met with Kevin, he was stoned. Very functionally high, he would reek of reefer no matter where or when you ran into him.

As a result, his constant craving for munchies would often be quelled with a quick visit to Tinti's, a restaurant on La Brea Boulevard, just south of Third Street. It was a short walk from Kevin's Hancock Park house, a stroll he took most evenings. In many ways it was the perfect hangout for Kevin. It had a full bar, a very authentic old world pizza and it did quite a brisk business despite being dark and almost somber. The bonus: Kevin wouldn't have to drive on those evenings when his elbow would bend a few too many times.

"If you didn't want to be seen, that was the place to go," Kevin would often muse. It astonished him that such an authentic old world pizza could be served in the midst of such faux Mediterranean décor. Plastic plants lined the booths. Old Chianti wine bottles collected dust on the window sills. You stepped back in time when you entered.

Mike Tinti, the proprietor and restaurant's namesake was a stereotypical, garrulous man in his early 50s. A bit rough around the edges, he definitely had the "hail fellow well met" attitude. You liked him in a "Sopranos" kind of way. He had the gift of mindless chatter, mid-level determination and "heard it all before" weariness. He could have been sent out from central casting to play any of a hundred supporting roles in *The Godfather*.

Working the kitchen for him was his son, Mike Jr. Easily the family wastrel. This 25-year-old was built like the brick shithouse—not fat, just someone you didn't want to mess with. It would take TNT to move him. Yet, you couldn't find a sweeter guy. He wasn't blessed with brains though. He gave "inept" a solid definition.

Kevin accused him as needing 10 minutes to button a pullover t-shirt.

Before very long, Kevin recognized that there were just too many pizzas being picked up for such a small business. And strangely everyone who called ahead was picking up the "Special." These pies were departing Tinti's like trains pulling out of Grand Central Station, one every couple of minutes. No way could Junior be preparing that many pizzas. He had trouble buckling his belt.

One afternoon, when Junior was ringing up a "Special" to-go order, Kevin noticed that the pizza box the customer picked up was devoid of any food. All that was inside was a small envelope.

Kevin called Junior over and asked him, "So, what makes the 'Special' pizza so special, Junior? I bet it's the toppings. What do you put on it?"

Junior was stumped. "Ah, everything?"

"Junior, that's a question. This isn't Jeopardy. I was looking for an answer." Kevin put him on the spot. He just walked away and moments later, Big Mike came over.

"Whatcha need?"

Kevin smiled, "I think I'd like a Special. How much?"

"That depends on the size," came his reply.

"A gram?"

Without missing a beat, Mike nodded, "C-note, cash. Two-fifty an eighth."

That's how Kevin discovered that all of his needs could be met from this one location. One-stop shopping—cocaine, grass, booze, oh, and pizza. How could you beat that?

Well, convenience and familiarity have its drawbacks. Kevin found himself constantly ordering the "Special" and beer. Over time, he found Tinti was also a shylock. He loaned money for high return. Though Kevin made a lot, he spent even more. He had a house with an elevator. He had a Cadillac with all the whistles and bells. He lavished gifts on everyone around him but his family. He bought friendships. He could spend hundreds on a Tiffany's money clip and immediately give it away—mostly because he never had any cash to keep in it.

Tinti was no fool. He knew how to exploit the situation. Soon Kevin found himself in some pretty deep debt. That's what the phone call was about to me that night. He had borrowed a modest sum, not paid it back in full and the interest grew. Interest—the vig became larger than the get—and Mike became tired of the excuses.

"C'mon, Kevin, he's not going to kill you for $2,000. If he did, he'd be out all that money. If you're dead, you can't pay him back." At least that was my comforting reasoning.

My partner indicated that it wasn't Tinti who wanted to kill him. It seems Kevin borrowed from another shark to pay Tinti who laid off some of the loan action which had reached $12,000 by this point. Mike Senior had been ordered by his regional "boss" to put the hit on. Senior wasn't going to do anything but what he was told.

The biggest indignity is that it was Mike Junior who would be carrying out the orders. It just didn't seem fair that Kevin, the guy who probably was the nicest to Junior, would be done in by the same person. Where was Vito or Giuseppe? Some *capo di tutti* or "made" man. "You gonna shoot me, get me the guy who got Bugsy Siegel. Why Junior?"

Mike only told Kevin about the order because he liked him. He wanted Kevin to have a chance to say good-bye to his family—his wife and three kids. That's some generosity. Though Kevin tried, he couldn't raise that kind of money and in the middle of a Sunday night. No banks were open. Bank cash machines had a max of $200 per day. So Kevin called me.

I certainly didn't have that kind of money hanging around my house. It was nearly two in the morning. Couldn't they wait until the banks opened just hours from then? Seems that Kevin tried that reasoning, but he also had insulted the regional "capo." Now there was a personal element to this hit.

I tried calling a few friends, apologizing for waking them in the middle of the night, asking if they had any cash. I couldn't go into the details so I just told them I needed it to get out of jail. I was able to raise a few thousand and got my wife to go pick it up. We had some emergency money at our Hollywood Hills house and added that to the kitty. While I went to the bank machines, my wife drove to our friends because I was supposed to be in jail. I couldn't come over and pick it up.

Finally I rendezvoused with my wife and though still $2,000 short; I delivered what I had to Mike Sr. He loan sharked me the gap money until the morning for a fee of $500. I had no choice. I took the terms.

There was another problem. I had to get to Tinti's boss with the cash and then get him to call off Junior and the hit. No one knew where to find Junior, and Kevin needed a place to hide out until I could get it all settled. So, putting ourselves in danger, my wife and I rented a motel room in our name in the San Fernando Valley, gave Kevin one of our cars so it couldn't be traced to him by the registration and set him up on the lamb.

I made the payment, but Junior's beeper battery had died. Even his father, after getting the message that the hit was off, couldn't stop his son. I called the motel and told Kevin the bad news that I couldn't find Junior to stop him. He took it surprisingly well and calmly suggested I go by 216 *South* Orange Drive and I might find the hit man there. But Kevin lived at 216 *North* Orange Drive. He assured me I would see Junior cruising by 216 South.

I'll be damned if Junior wasn't so stupid that he got the North and South mixed up, just as Kevin had thought. I found and intercepted Junior. Using my cellphone, I got his father on the line, and Mike Junior was called off.

Kevin was safe. I was out all this money which Kevin never did pay me back. My friends all wanted to know why I had been arrested so, being a writer, I made up a story. For a while after that, I lived in fear of knowing too much about the LA mob scene. Fortunately, Kevin never borrowed again from Tinti.

But I wasn't stupid. I could see the writing on the wall. I realized either being a writer/producer was a tremendously dangerous job in this town or the partnership I had aligned myself with was starting to become way too risky. Either way, I had some serious decisions to make.

*****

Now, today, as I sit in my office almost 20 years later, I have some serious decisions to make as well. They too deal with life and death. Kevin's future right now is in the hands of his doctors. My future will be determined by a malfunctioning liver. Maybe Kevin and I will be back together sometime soon at that big writers' table in the sky. Who knows...?

I still haven't gotten a call from Helen. So for now, I'm just going to put the Tinti's menu in the save pile and continue my spring clean-up while I continue to wait for some news.

GOING TO BANKS

To what extent would you go to win a bet? What if the point of the challenge was only a wager over what is the best beer someone ever tasted?

Well to prove Kevin's point, we went to Barbados by way of Warner Bros. Features. Looking back, I can say it was all worth it. When all was said and done, this adventure was as interesting as the movie we sold in order to make this escapade happen. It all started with a pitch meeting.

We were in between gigs in the mid-1980s. Somewhere tucked inside the Los Angeles Times was a small article about a tax loophole that existed, and many people were taking advantage of it. Married couples would get divorced in late December and then remarry after the first of the New Year. In doing so, they were able to capitalize on this obscure loophole, lowering their tax liability substantially. Some people, obviously those making large sums of money, could save thousands. It actually paid for their Christmas vacation. So when all was said and done, the couple was married, divorced, got a paid vacation, then remarried and put some money in the bank as well. Isn't our tax system great?!

And so that loophole begot *Divorce and Consent*. We came up with a wispy, romantic comedy TV movie to pitch. It was based on fact—always a good place to start.

We had an "in" at Warner Bros. through our agent to Lorimar, the TV company responsible for a number of movies of the week, some which became hit series like *The Waltons*, *Eight is Enough* and *Dallas*. And Lorimar was also just starting to dabble in TV comedy with *Perfect Strangers* and *Full House*. So they seemed like as good a place as any to try it out.

James (not Jim or Jimmy or Jimbo or Jimaroony) Lassiter was the vice president in their TV movie department. The executive popped the door open to his inner office, and then lead us into his private domain. It was, to say the least, an artistically decorated workplace. Kevin took it all in, looked at James and with a polite smile commented, "Gay, huh?"

The vice president smiled. "Boyfriend decorated it. I'd have gone a bit more butch."

I didn't know exactly how to respond to that, but Kevin just continued on as if this was normal parlor conversation. "That's what you get when you let a bottom have a studio decorator's budget... I'm surprised you don't have some frilly lampshades."

James retorted, "Have enough of those at home."

Before we started our pitch, we went through the general small talk. One thing led to another and not surprisingly, the conversation led once again to Kevin having served in the Merchant Marines. I sensed trouble when he offered, "You know the gay Merchant Marine's motto, don't you? 'Never leave your buddies behind.'" Kevin was ahead of his time—politically incorrect before the term was created.

I immediately drove the conversation to our TV movie pitch. I thought that was wise under the circumstances. James indicated he was ready to hear it. Then, in as effeminate an affectation as you could possibly imagine, he shot us: "So, what have you boys got for me?

I think that was James' way of saying he was okay with Kevin's gay remarks, so we scrambled and told him our story. He loved it which made us feel pretty good. Then he sort of took the wind out of our sails.

"I think it's too good for an MOW." Then he added after a very pregnant pause, "I think it's a fuckin' feature."

"Now that's a first," Kevin shared. "I never wrote a question for a game show and someone said, 'That's too good a question. Let's turn it into a series.'"

James went on. "Look, I'm serious. This would make a great movie and I'm going to prove it to you. Lorimar just set up a feature division with Warners. Let me take you down there."

We walked down the corridor of this old executive building on the Warner Bros. lot. Somehow, during the conversation along the way, it came out that James' passion was beer. I would have thought chintz window coverings or Broadway musicals, but shame on me.

Now beer was something Kevin was an expert in. Though truthfully, he was always knowledgeable in any subject at any time we attended a meeting. He was amazing that way. From art to literature, sports and music, travel and foreign destinations. I don't know where it came from, but he had that knack of knowing just enough about everything to impress anyone. With James and beer, this was one true connoisseur talking to another.

They spoke of everything from ales to lagers, stouts to pilsners, porters to bocks—traditional or the German doppelbock. It was all chatter to me but it was Gustav Mahler to Kevin's ears. He knew each country's brew, the brands, the alcohol content. This was a conversation that would be more appropriate or expected in the Munich Hofbrauhaus then the halls of Warner Bros. Film Studios; the haunts of Jimmy Cagney, Humphrey Bogart, and Edward G. Robinson.

The walk took 30 seconds; the conversation, 10 minutes. I just smiled and nodded. To me a beer was a brewski, and I didn't care for it much anyway. These guys were totally immersed into it.

Soon the chatter veered toward the best beer either of them ever had. James named one I never heard —Westvleterenof. It's made by Belgium monks. They only sell a few cases each year outside the monastery and at over a 100 bucks a bottle. Kevin said he had tasted it, and James was wrong. "The best tasting beer in the world was Banks Beer, and it's only sold in Barbados—50 cents a bottle."

They went back and forth which led to a $10 bet. The only problem was that the Banks Beer was not pasteurized, so at that time it was prohibited from being distributed into the States. James told Kevin he'd have a hard time proving it, then. Kevin wrapped that up with, "Leave that to me. Ten bucks?" They shook on it.

We were ushered into the new offices of the feature division. There Harlan Thomas, an English gentleman of dignified qualities, was introduced to us by James, who said, "Harlan, these guys just pitched me the best feature idea I ever heard."

Harlan looked at his assistant, an amazingly attractive and well-endowed young woman, who told her boss that his next appointment wasn't for another hour. James insisted that Harlan see us right away, so we were shown into his office. Kevin commented on his selection of secretaries to which Harlan, with all his British dignity commented, "My, but she does have a marvelous set of cans, doesn't she?"

That expression, "marvelous set of cans" coming from his mouth just seemed so Monty Python-ish. After a brief background summary, we launched into our story. "It's called, *Divorce and Consent*." Harlan loved the title. Kevin said we could stop right there, and he could buy it—"Save us all a lot of time."

He indicated for us to continue. Kevin was his usual outgoing self, making all kinds of divorce jokes, travel jokes, British humor quips. In general, he told the story briefly but entertained greatly. Kevin's pitch boiled down to this logline: Utilizing a tax loophole, a happily married couple of 10 years, amicably divorce, go on a vacation together in the Bahamas. Now single, they become attracted to others, jealousies arise, and they end up competing for each other, falling in love all over again.

Short. Sweet. Devoid of many details. That left a lot of room for Kevin's comedy runs and riffs. Once again, it was met with a vivid and positive reaction. All and all, a great, if unexpected meeting.

By the time we got back to our houses, we had a call from Herb. Lorimar Features was buying our movie. Kevin told the agent to negotiate in a trip to Barbados for research.

"Barbados? In our pitch they went to the Bahamas."

Kevin shrugged, "They'll never know the difference. Besides, they don't have Banks Beer in the Bahamas."

Two weeks later, we were heading off to Barbados. I was in the shower getting ready to leave when the phone rang. My wife answered. It was Peter Bart, the president of Lorimar Features. He said he just saw a copy of our deal memo and realized we were going to Barbados on their money. He wanted to know why? When I got out of the shower I called him back and had to re-pitch the movie concept substituting Barbados for the Bahamas. He actually liked it and wished us well.

The time Kevin and I spent in Barbados was a lot of fun. Our resort was 15 minutes outside of the capital city of Bridgetown, so it was quiet and laid back—just like the rest of the island. From my standpoint, it was one of the most beautiful places on earth.

A trip to the Banks Beer Brewery was a must stop. We sampled the fresh brew there and though I'm sure it was good, I didn't really notice the intricacies or the subtleties of the flavor or the brewing process. Kevin loaded up the trunk of our rental car with about five cases, and we were on our way.

Now to say "on our way" is a bit misleading. Sugar-cane fields filled the inner sections of the island. They were tall like corn fields and you couldn't see anything much, left or right, unless you were driving along the coast. Think of driving in a maze of corn. Streets weren't marked. If you wanted to give directions, you'd tell someone to go three fields down, go right immediately after the church, when you see the second cane field, go right again.

And so we found our trip back to the resort very challenging and ultimately got lost. We asked for directions from the locals and kept getting farther and farther from our destination. It wasn't a language problem. It was us attempting to follow directions, trying to pay attention to driving on the opposite side of the road and a general buzz from the Banks Beer.

Finally we turned onto a narrow road, only to find out it was a long driveway, not a street. When we reached the house at the end, a rather nice residence, Kevin decided he needed to pee. So he got out of the car, went around the side of the house to take care of his business. Suddenly we heard a woman's voice calling over, "Why don't you come inside and use the bathroom?"

What a friendly offer; I decided I'd go with Kevin. We didn't yet see the woman, just her open screen door. It was darker inside so we just kind of nodded as we entered. This elderly woman indicated the location of the restroom.

While Kevin went in first, I smiled, introduced myself and thanked the woman for her generosity. I told her we had been driving around for about an hour, trying to get back to our resort. She said she knew what that was like. She was an American ex-patriot who moved to the serenity of the island years ago. She still had problems navigating her way around. "They say they're going to someday add street signs," she added with a kind smile. "Doubt I'll live to see that!"

She offered me something to drink. She hadn't been to the store recently but could make me some tea. Before I could answer, Kevin returned holding a statue in his hands.

"Is this yours?" he asked the woman.

"Yes. I know it must seem strange to keep it in the powder room."

It was an Oscar, an Academy Award statuette. I'd never seen one in person. Kevin nodded to the woman, "Miss Colbert, I'm Kevin Hartigan."

And so started our chance meeting with Claudette Colbert. What a wondrous woman she turned out to be. And we were here in her house, just us and her. No pretenses. No airs.

She asked what we were doing on the island. When we told her we were writer/producers doing research for a movie we'd be shooting in Barbados, she was so intrigued. It was like a little return visit to her past.

We sat and did have tea together. Kevin invited her to enjoy one of our many bottles of Banks from the trunk of the car, but this demure woman passed on the offer. We begged her to let us take her out to dinner, to continue our conversation. She declined, telling us she doesn't like going out anymore.

She gave us directions how to get back to the resort which she had never visited, but heard was very plush. "Something like the old bungalows at the Beverly Hills Hotel, I'd imagine." She recalled some stories about being at the Polo Lounge, then poolside with Gable and Lombard. "That's before they were out as a couple," she confided. "Gable as still married at that time, you know. Kind of scandalous back then."

Now, if nothing else, this trip was amazing. When we got back home, we couldn't wait to start writing up our story outline because we wanted to return to the island as soon as we could. We even planned a small cameo scene we hoped Miss Colbert would agree to do, though we knew that was kind of a longshot.

Eventually a box was delivered to us on the lot. Actually it was more of a crate which was sent out from Barbados. While I was opening it, Kevin was calling James, his beer buddy from Lorimar and telling him to drop whatever he was doing, or whoever he was doing. James and Kevin still had the playful "gay" banter thing going. "Get your ass, if it's not occupied, over here right away.

And bring your $10…" There was a beat, then, "No, it's not for a blow job." This is what I had to put up with.

When I got the crate opened, there was a pile of Kevin's clothes and under it was a case of Banks Beer. Kevin had arranged with someone at the hotel to have it shipped to us. Somehow it made it through customs. I guess if you pay enough, you can get anything into this country.

James and Kevin were busy into their brews. I was telling the Lorimar exec about Claudette Colbert's Oscar when Peter Bart, Lorimar's film president, summoned us down to his office. We had never met him but I had spoken to him on the phone before our trip.

Peter seemed a bit agitated as he shoved a few invoices into our hands and asked us to explain these charges. This was our hotel invoice which was directly billed to the studio. The problems weren't with the room charges, the car rental or even some of the incidentals: it was the bar tab. It was more than $4,000. Peter lividly exploded, "I can't believe this amount!"

Kevin was puzzled as well, "I'm with you there, Peter. I thought it would have been much higher."

I explained that each evening, while meeting and interviewing the people at the resort, all for background for the movie, we'd graciously thank them by buying some drinks. Peter said there weren't that many people on the island for that many drinks. "But," I added, "we did get together with Claudette Colbert and we might be able to get her in the movie."

Peter just shook his head and told Kevin to pay the bill himself. He wouldn't authorize it. Kevin asked him if he was sure he wouldn't reconsider. Our answer was, we were shown to the door.

Back in the office, James was still there. He wanted to know what the boss called us in for. Kevin made up some story about wanting to know how we made out on our trip. The television exec surprised me and Kevin when he started for the door with two unopened bottles of the Banks Beer. He was going to take them home for his boyfriend. James smiled, conceded that the Banks Beer was the best and told Kevin his $10 from the bet was on the desk. As James reached the door, Kevin reminded him that they weren't twist off tops. James chuckled and with a wink, "They may not twist off, but as my power bottom boyfriend will tell you, they do twist in." These two were sick men.

Once we had the office back to ourselves, I asked Kevin if he was going to pay the bill. Did I need to contribute or what? Kevin had it all under control, so he claimed. He had a letter to write. I went back to work on what they were paying us for, our "Divorce and Consent" movie.

A few days later we showed up at the studio as usual. We were just about to do a final pass on the first draft of the script when Peter summoned us back to his office again. He was holding a letter from the US State Department, on their official stationary.

Peter read it aloud, "Thank you Lorimar Pictures for generously and graciously loaning us the entertaining services of your writers, David and Kevin, while in Barbados. I only wish my boss, President Reagan, had the opportunity to laugh and enjoy the evening as much as I did. Signed, Alexander Haig, Secretary of State." Peter stared at us. "Is this for real?"

"Go call Alex yourself if you don't believe it," Kevin puffed. "You'll like him. He's a great guy, the general. He's the real reason the bill was so high. Fucker drinks like a fish."

"And only the good stuff," I added. "Plus he had two staff."

The suspicious company president wanted to know why we didn't say anything about this before. Kevin said he didn't want the secretary's reputation to be tarnished.

Peter thought about it for a minute. He picked up the phone and I was relieved when it turned out he was calling accounting, not the State Department. He authorized them to pay the entire Barbados bill, including the questioned bar tab. Then he turned to us, "This better be one hell of a movie."

A movie sale. A free trip to Barbados. Tea with an Oscar winner. A triumphant beer bet. A forged letter from the secretary of state. Talk about your Hollywood fairytale.

END OF FRIES

Our deal with Chuck Fries was coming to a natural close–an unusual occurrence since we tended to be unceremoniously fired from most of our jobs. Chuck was considering keeping us on for an additional year, despite all of the hassles and attacks Kevin had made on him, his son Butch and Malcolm Stuart, still the company's development maven. When the boss called us in on this particular Wednesday, we figured it was either to fire us or to rehire us. As we hadn't done anything too much out of the ordinary, lately, it was the latter. He wanted to discuss an extension. The news was symphonic music to my ears; a crazy out of tune street cacophony to Kevin's.

"Why?" was Kevin's immediate response. "We've been with you for years; don't you think it's about time we moved on?"

Now if you were to ask Malcolm, he'd surely say "yes." Butch certainly would echo that notion loud and clear after all the abuse he took from us. If you were to get into Chuck's head, you'd see a different calculation. We had made money for him. We surely had made money for us. The difference is Chuck was an owner. We were employees.

Kevin suggested that for us to consider staying on, we should get a piece of the company. Butch, the negotiator for the production house, chimed in that we already got percentages of our shows. But Kevin wanted more. He wanted a piece of the entire CFP pie. He wanted a taste from every show they produced. Kevin felt we helped build the company's reputation with our irreverent personalities and prolific pilot sales. He wasn't greedy—he just wanted a few percent. "We'll even forgo our salary. How's that for good faith?"

That was a non-starter for Chuck. Butch did make a nice opening offer for us to stay on for an additional year. What he did in reality was just cause Kevin to start the rock tumbling down from the top of the mountain. That rock picked up speed and caused devastation on the way down.

"Chuck, how can you surround yourself like this? Four Fries relatives on the payroll. You know what they say, 'families are like fudge...mostly sweet, with a few nuts.' In your case you just got the recipe backwards."

Kevin negotiated from intimidation. His strength was his true willingness to walk away. Sometimes strength and stupidity are the same things. This was heading in the latter's direction.

Kevin told Butch and his father that the last time an indentured servitude deal like the one Butch just offered was accepted, the Mayflower was still tied to Plymouth Rock. We needed a piece of the company.

"That ain't gonna happen. So let's move from there," Chuck bellowed.

Kevin changed tack. He went from passive aggressive to just plain aggressive. "You know, Chuck, it's nice to see that the success we helped you achieve hasn't changed you much. You're still the same ass you used to be—only three sizes larger. Look around you... You're surrounded by your son and your lackey. Imbeciles... Why? So you'll be the smartest one in the trio?

"I've heard enough," cautioned Chuck.

"You know, Chuck, you trust your son here. But you want to know what his plans are for you? When you die, he's going to bury you upside down so you can see where you're going."

"Get out of here. Now!"

We got up and started to walk out. Chuck shouted to us that our services there were no longer needed. We were through.

Kevin smiled and shot back. "The only thing you'll regret more than this is looking in the mirror – You'll see the kind of guy you'd really like to run into sometime— when he's walking and you're driving a car!"

Well, he had done it again. We crossed to our office, went to the closet and pulled out some boxes. We started packing when Butch popped his head in and asked for our security cards back to the lot. Kevin handed it to him and said "Here's the pass. The 'Omen only' parking is on the left. It's the spot with the three sixes."

As we put our stuff into boxes, I asked Kevin what we were going to do now. He assured me, as he had so many times before, he'd take care of it. I was tired of hearing that.

We now had just walked away after our third year of our deal with the Chuck Fries Company. Kevin had grown restless. Our projects, one by one were failing to catch on. Kevin's antics were becoming much more of a thorn in people's sides. His novelty was wearing off. Part of that was because of boredom. Part was because he was becoming more vicious in his attacks. For so long he had gotten away with things. And with each success, he kept biting off just a little bit more, taking a few additional risks and chances. He became ever gradually, more of an aggressor than a salesman. He hadn't lost his comedy talent. He lost his sense of humanity. Dr. Frankenstein would have remarked as he did looking upon his monster, "It's alive!"

These ever-growing serious antics not only wore on the industry as a whole, but it took its toll on our relationship. On three of our previous firings, the employers actually said, "Kevin, you're fired. David, if you'd like to stay on, we'd gladly have you."

But Kevin couldn't accept that. He'd shoot back, without even consulting me first, "If you keep David and let me go, I'll file an anti-trust suit against you for breaking up our team." The last time he took that tack, he even had the chutzpah to tell them, "When I get through with you the sign over the front gate to the lot will read, The Hartigan-Warner Bros. Studio... in that order!"

That of course left me in the middle. I didn't like being fired. It hurt. A lot. Being asked to stay stroked my ego and really made me feel good. I also had a part of me that said I had achieved all of my success because of Kevin, maybe even despite him. I couldn't walk out on him. As strong as he projected himself, he was also vulnerable—he just hid it well. Astoundingly, each time I walked out with him I failed to realize the harm it was doing to my career, my family and my future. It also stoked bolder and more extreme brashness within him.

I didn't know how much longer or how many more times I could take this. I was uneasy and quietly simmering. I was contemplating getting out before my choices were gone. To this point, basically all my career decisions had been made for me, by Kevin. Now, after this latest tirade, I wasn't sure of a lot of things. Walking away takes great strength and confidence. I didn't know if I had those—yet.

VIACOM DIOS

Within two days we were back on the CBS Studio Center lot; but not with Chuck Fries or his company. Herb Karp and the folks at the William Morris Agency had talked to the people over at Viacom, and we took a meeting over there. They knew of us, and were considering adding us to their ever growing talent roster of writer/producers. Hell, the whole town knew of us—it was becoming more of, could they stomach us? Creatively yes. Personally no. With a push from the agency, the Viacom honchos agreed to have a meet and greet.

The inevitable question came around to why, after three years and a vast number of pilot sales, we were no longer with Chuck Fries Productions.

Without missing a beat, Kevin said Fries just can't handle the truth. This, by the way, was five years before Nicholson made that phrase so popular in the film *A Few Good Men*. But once you opened the door to Kevin, he burst through. He went on that Chuck gets carried away with his own self-importance.

"Unfortunately, not far away enough! Of course moving him requires a forklift and a few strong men."

I attempted to soften the personal attacks a bit. Chuck really was relatively patient with us and our antics. We weren't angels, after all. Yet a kind word for anyone who'd fired us would never come from Kevin. At this point in our career, that meant there weren't going to be kind words for very many.

"And is he ever cheap. Money means *nothing* to him. Ask him for some, that's what you get—*nothing*." Kevin was having a moment. With a saner person, it would be called a meltdown.

He probably could have gone on for hours when he got wound up like this, but he had Dick Reisberg, the head of Viacom, chuckling away to the point of Reisberg offering us an overall deal. I never knew if it was because he truly wanted us, or because he liked the idea that he got us away from Chuck. But it didn't matter. Once again, Kevin and I were locked into a very nice financial deal and with a very influential company.

Coincidentally, we were on the same lot as Chuck, just one building down. We were given offices that had been specially built for Amanda Blake when she starred on the long running television series, *Gunsmoke*. It used to be shot on this lot, along with a number of other shows—*Gilligan's Island*, *The Mary Tyler Moore Show*, *Alice*, and later on, *Roseanne* and *Seinfeld*.

Our office space included a fantastic sitting area, dressing area, and a magnificent bathroom with our own steam room. The private shower had etched glass, sliding doors, one had, "Miss" written on it and the other "Kitty." Kevin wanted to take them when we left—he collected odd pieces of Hollywood memorabilia. I cautioned him to wait until we finished our run there. I didn't want to give Viacom a good reason to fire us—and theft would certainly qualify.

About a week after setting up shop, we made our first television sale for Viacom. It was at ABC, over in Century City. The show was from an idea I had that Kevin never let me pitch. He finally relented and actually loved it, once he got his fingers into it—*Ben of Beacon Hill.*

It was about a young, newly married couple who move into an old brownstone in Boston's Beacon Hill district. The husband is an inventor. He goes down in the basement to his workshop one day and his most recent time-travel invention blows up. When the smoke clears, standing there is a young, Benjamin Franklin, also an inventor. Their experiments crisscrossed and here he is. The series is about the newlywed couple with a boarder, Ben Franklin; they are trying to get him back to his own time. While there in the 1980s, Ben picks up ideas he'll bring back when he returns to the late 1700s. The twist that Kevin put on it was that our 20-something Ben Franklin would be like Jack Benny—the mannerisms, the style and the stingy humor. Kevin had the perfect guy to play the part. It was David Agress.

On *Happy Days*, David was a guest star in the infamous Fonzie "jumping the shark" episode where he played his role just like a young Jack Benny. David had his walk. His delivery. His whole presence. And I have to say that in writing the pilot, it made it so easy because we could "hear" David/Jack/Ben's voice and personality.

We actually arranged to meet with David before we wrote the script to see if he was interested and available. Of course he was. He wasn't a big name and what a compliment for two well-known Hollywood producers wanting you for a series leading role that's yet to be written. As soon as David said yes, Kevin made a cardinal sin. He promised the gig to David. He didn't bother to check with Viacom or ABC first. Kevin knew they'd flip over and fall in love with David Agress. The stage was set.

A FINAL WORD

I was writing up the final pass on the script for the pilot for *Ben of Beacon Hill* in our offices at Viacom and I could sense it was really in good shape. Kevin decided that while I was plying my skills "polishing the gold," he had something that he wanted to do. He'd been sneaking away from the lot every day for a few hours. I didn't give it much thought because he was there when I needed him. But curiosity got the best of me.

"You want to know where I go? C'mon with me."

We hopped into Kevin's car and drove over the hill. Within about 15 minutes we had pulled into the parking lot at Cedars-Sinai Hospital in West Hollywood. Shortly thereafter, we were at the foot of a patient's bed—our friend Snag. I hardly recognized him. He was fighting diabetes, and losing. He'd had a leg removed, was blind, and was hardly more than some loosely fitting tissue covering some bones.

I asked Kevin why he hadn't told me. He just looked at me and said, "I know how sensitive you are. I didn't know if you could take it."

Kevin was right. Things like this were very difficult for me. Kevin, as he usually did, went out of his way to protect me from the difficulties in life. I know deep down he felt I was soft and couldn't handle certain inevitabilities. But I can. Truth is if I hadn't been let in on this I would have felt robbed, cheated and resentful. Certainly I didn't want to ever see this kind of horrific apparition, but I would never have forgiven Kevin if he hadn't brought me. I owed this fine gentleman my chance to comfort him.

I will grant Kevin this—even now, I don't really understand the bond he shared with Snag. It had no words to describe it. As vile and detestable as some of Kevin's actions were—and I know they were—there was this other side. And it was demonstrated to only two people that I know of, including his family. It was shared with Snag and with me.

Kevin pulled up a chair and moved to the side of the bed. He took Snag's hand or more aptly skeletal appendage and gently stroked it. He seemed to sense someone was there.

"It's us, Kevin and David. Can you hear us, Snag?" Kevin gently whispered into his ear.

"I'm dying, not deaf." Ever feisty Snag. He wasn't leaving without a fight. "Did you bring me anything?"

From out of his briefcase, Kevin pulled a bottle of Four Roses single barrel bourbon. He unscrewed the top, assisted Snag to an inclined position, and put the bottle to his lips. Snag reached out for it, tilted the bottle up and took a swig. "Where's David?" he asked as Kevin lowered him to the pillow.

"I'm right here, Snag." I went over and took his other hand. I held it between both of mine. There was nothing there. These fingers that had pounded out some of the most memorable lines in show business now were but thin slivers of bone covered with loose, ill-fitting, skin gloves.

Then Snag slowly started to tell us a story he told us many times before. Hardly a sentence into it, his words became mumbles. His awareness drifted away; his eyes fluttered, then shut. Even though Snag most likely couldn't hear a word, that didn't stop Kevin. For almost an hour, I heard Kevin regale this unconscious man with what was happening at the studios, in the town of Hollywood and with names of people so old, probably only Snag would have known them. Kevin's stories and jokes were so right on. If only Snag could hear them.

Finally, I couldn't take it any longer. I asked Kevin for his keys. He told me we should both go. We had work to do.

"You hang in there, Snag. We'll be back to see you tomorrow." Those words didn't conjure any movement. The machines said our buddy was alive, but his actions didn't confirm it. Yet almost amazingly, as we were walking out, Snag started talking again— the same story he began before he drifted off. I looked at Kevin. He couldn't leave and neither could I. We stayed for a few more minutes until Snag drifted again, but not before Kevin had helped him to one more shot of liquor.

In Hollywood, death is your friend. Everybody turns out. They talk about you in positive terms as if you were there listening. At one funeral Kevin and I attended, Kevin caught a producer, sitting down front, turning around and looking about. I asked Kevin what he thought she was doing. "Counting the house," came his response. Yes, death was like a holiday gathering. Family and friends. You were judged by the number and quality of the turnout.

The final curtain dropped for Snag Werris on February 27, 1987. It was Kevin's sincerest request of the family that he be given the privilege of delivering the eulogy. They had no idea what they were in for. What Kevin did next changed the sendoff business forever. George Jessel was known for delivering celebrity eulogies until he had passed a year earlier. Jessel once gave a stirring eulogy, eloquent and laudatory; then, while concluding, looked down at the open casket, and remarked, "Oh, my God. I know this man." So perhaps eulogies aren't as genuine as we'd like to believe. What Kevin did this day must have made George Jessel turn over in his grave...twice.

What follows is the eulogy that Kevin delivered:

First, to the Werris family, I want to thank you for allowing me to address everyone on this somber occasion. I feel particularly honored. On their behalf, I want to thank you all for coming. Yesterday, Snag's three daughters lost a father and comedy lost a landmark. Getting Snag here today wasn't all that easy. For starters, he had to die, and believe me, he had done that on stage so many times before, he almost slept through his cue.

Many of you might not know this, but Snag is the man who created "The Hokey Pokey." That's right. That "Hokey Pokey." The most traumatic part for his undertaker was getting him prepared for his sendoff. They put his left foot in. He put his left foot out... And then the trouble started.

Snag's career included working on a number of Disney shows and as a result, he requested that his pallbearers today include the Seven Dwarfs—of old age: Itchy, Bitchy, Sweaty, Bloated, Gassy and Forgetful. When I told him that was only six and there were supposed to be seven, he said see number six again. Forgetful.

Forgetful. I can't be forgetful. Not of the efforts of this man. When I went to his apartment the last time, I used his powder room where he still had a sign...

GUESTS ARE ASKED TO REFRAIN FROM DISPOSING OF THEIR CIGARETTE BUTTS IN THE URINAL AS THEY BECOME SOGGY AND DIFFICULT FOR ME TO LIGHT.

Snag not only was a smoker, but he loved to drive. What many of you don't know is that despite Snag's vision being a constant problem for him, he still got behind the wheel from time to time. One day his daughter Wendy called him in the car. "Dad," she said, "on the news they just reported that there's a car going the wrong way on the 101 Freeway. Please be careful!" Over the receiver she heard some swerving sounds and some honking, followed by her father yelling, "It's not just one car, it's hundreds of them!"

Upon Snag's passing, I came across the earliest piece Snag had written. I'm not going into his age but when I said written, I misspoke. They were chiseled. And we all know what a prolific chiseler he was. I thought I'd share this story with you so you could get a better idea of the kind of brilliant mind he had.

This story was autobiographical, according to the Rosetta Stone which was found next to this tablet. Seems Snag came across quite a beautiful young New York woman, before he met his late wife, Charlotte. This goes back just before the war. This woman was so depressed that she decided to end her life by throwing herself off the dock and into the ocean. "Wait!" shouted young Snag. "You have so much to live for." He joined her. "My name's Snag, I'm a sailor, and I'm off to Europe tomorrow. Let me stow you away on my ship. I'll take care of you, bring you food every day, and keep you happy." With nothing to lose, combined with the fact that she had always wanted to go to Europe, the young woman accepted. That night Snag smuggled her aboard and hid her in a lifeboat. Every night he would bring her sandwiches and then make love to her until dawn. Three weeks later she was discovered by the captain during a routine inspection."

"What are you doing here?" asked the captain. "I have an arrangement with Snag, one of your sailors," she replied. "He brings food and I get a free trip to Europe." "I see," the captain responded. "Plus," she added, "He's screwing me."

"I'll say he is," replied the captain. "This is the Staten Island Ferry."

I'm sure Snag would tell you that was a true story. But there's only one true story today. We're all going to miss you, buddy. And when you get up to heaven, remember to keep God laughing. He's heard all of Groucho's jokes already.

And now, if I can ask all of you to please rise one final time, put your hands together and let's give Snag that final standing ovation he so richly deserves.

The entire assembly did just that. The faces of Snag's family, coupled with the bravura of Kevin for sending our friend off in what would have certainly made him happy, echoes to this day in memoriam.

A thought of that event brings me back to today. Was Kevin going to be joining his old friend soon? Or had he gone already and Helen just hadn't gotten around to giving me the call? I looked at my phone for a second. I was thankful for the device not yet ringing. I didn't think I was ready for that call—unless of course it was good news that Kevin would pull through. I did something I hadn't done in a very long time. I found a small amount of marijuana in one of the boxes I was cleaning out. I also found a pipe. I filled it, smoked it, and relaxed again as I awaited some word.

KEVIN JUMPS THE SHARK

We sent the first draft of the script *Ben of Beacon Hill* to Viacom. They loved it, turning it immediately over to ABC. Within two days we heard back. They too loved it and wanted us to come in for a meeting to discuss a second draft.

Once we got to ABC in Century City, we mentioned that we wanted David Agress for the part of young Ben. As a matter of fact, he lived right around the corner from the office building. We could call and see if he would come over so the group could meet him. They agreed. David said he would be right there. Then we looked out the window. Sure as shit, we saw that Jack Benny patented walk and arm swing as David made his way across Century Park East to the ABC building. Everyone in the room was smiling. We had a great find on our hands. As Kevin gave us a minute of his own Jack Benny impression ending in "Gee, fellas, what do you think?" David was shown into the office.

We had a short meet and greet. David was, just as we expected, perfect. He left almost as quickly as he came in, not wanting to overstay his welcome, something a lot of actors would be well-advised to learn. Kevin told David we'd catch up with him in the lobby. "Wait for us. We'll be right out."

As soon as he was gone, Kevin shot everyone in the room a playful look. "Tell me this guy isn't the next Mork from *Mork and Mindy*? He's got that special Robin Williams quality for this role, doesn't he?"

That really made the executives in the room think. There was an actual silence so powerful that you'd swear you could hear the cogs of wheels turning. Then the vice president of the network said, "We sure could use another *Mork and Mindy*."

"Now you're getting our picture," Kevin beamed with a relieved sigh.

"Think we can get Robin Williams to come back and do Ben?" That was the network honcho's question.

Kevin argued that we don't need Robin Williams. We've got our Ben right in the lobby—Agress.

But the Viacom guys and the ABC guys were already sold—on the wrong guy. The network brass turned to us, "You're on the air for 13 if you get us Williams."

"But I already made a commitment to David. We can't dump him. I gave him my word." Kevin and I were crushed. Just moments before they loved this guy and the whole idea.

"Offer him some other role. The neighbor. Or the wife's brother. Just not Ben. We want Robin in that role... He'll kill in it."

Kevin and I left, went to the lobby and sat, flanking David. He was anxious and like most young actors, insecure. "How did I do?"

"You did great," Kevin shared with him. "They loved you." Then after a short beat. "It's us that didn't do so well."

We could see the heavy weight on David's face and shoulders. "They passed on the show," Kevin untruthfully confided. "They aren't going to do it."

Rather than go back on his word, Kevin chose to walk away from the meeting, from the building and from the show. And we did. We got in to the elevator and took it down to the street with David, who sadly, we would never see again.

Now the truth is that we probably couldn't have gotten Robin Williams anyway. He was a rising feature star and a regular on *Saturday Night Live*. But once again the surprising side of Kevin reared up. If he gave his word, he kept it. You may have hated him for it, but a promise made was a promise kept. He didn't make many, but his word was truly his bond.

This didn't go over well at Viacom. Within two weeks they had us fired and removed from the lot. We were bought out. The word spread fast of our latest insubordination. Of course, the real reason wasn't discussed. Agress never was told the truth. That just wasn't Kevin's way of doing things. But this show, *Ben of Beacon Hill,* was the last show Kevin and I sold together; the last script that we wrote together.

Partnerships don't die easily. Ours was no exception. The official dissolution was yet to come, but the writing was on the wall. Actually this brings me to one of the last misadventures Kevin would involve me in.

During our final day on the Viacom lot, I helped Kevin smuggle the two etched-glass shower doors from our office into the Tinti's Restaurant pizza delivery truck. Amanda Blake's dressing room's

"Miss" and "Kitty" doors were about to go missing. They would reside with Kevin until he finally left Hollywood.

BEGINNING OF THE END

After our dismissal from Viacom, just one of a number of firings and removals from what was a career of opportunities, mostly squandered; I had some soul searching to do. I had spent about ten years or so, living in the long shadows of a man who taught me so much—and mostly learned the hard way. It all came with a price.

The comedy brand of Hartigan and Garber, which around Hollywood was once synonymous with cutting edge, off their rocker, outrageous, pushing the envelope, wildly original, even genius, had perished. Once again, we had gone down in flames. Only now we had gained the reputation in Hollywood as being impossible to work with. Brash. Cocky. Self-centered. Egotistical. Abrasive. Those were the kind terms. We were referred to and thought of as pariahs, plague carriers and much worse.

In the words of Dylan Thomas, "Do not go gentle into that good night." Unfortunately, we had already passed over the threshold. We were now, in the vernacular of the industry, D.O.A.

Our mutual friend, Emmy winning writer, Art Baer, phrased it best when told of a Kevin production deal, "Don't worry, he'll burn that bridge when he gets it." And he was right—and most likely Kevin and I had both burned our bridges.

Sometimes knowing when to get off the bus is as important as knowing where to get on. I had grabbed at the brass ring on the Hollywood merry-go-round many times. With Kevin's assistance, I emerged victoriously each lap. This was different.

The constant firings and fights with higher ups had taken its toll. I had a wife, a home in the Hollywood Hills and we wanted to start a family. With Kevin by my side and calling most of the shots, there was constant uncertainty. He was, for lack of a better analogy, like having an ex-wife who calls you daily insisting still on having everything her way.

I was finally at the tipping point. I was never going to be the talent that Kevin was. Those special people come around about as often as Halley's Comet. Yet, I certainly was no longer a neophyte. I had been in some miraculous battles and came out alive. I witnessed great events, I participated in calamitous adventures and I tasted success along with some abject failures. After years of being in the shotgun seat of the car, I wanted to drive my own career. I wasn't sure how hard that would be and really didn't find out until later the extent of those burdens and challenges. I had truly been in a protected environment. I resided in the Kevin bubble.

So I found myself unhappy, unfulfilled and anxious. Being tethered to Kevin always seemed to bring me bobbing back up until we landed the next fish. How much longer until I became "the old man and the sea," fighting incurable bad luck, risky choices and engaging in a series of relentlessly agonizing skirmishes?

Labor conflicts are never good for either side. In the mid-1980s the Writers Guild of America called an industry-wide strike. At the same time, an opportunity did come my way. I was offered a job as a tour chaperone to accompany a group of 30 people to Asia for a month. Not only would I be getting to see far off lands, I would be paid as well. It was a break; a chance to get away. With a strike going on, I would not be able to earn any money from writing or producing unless the guild settled the work stoppage. There was no way to know how long the strike would last. So I told Kevin about my opportunity and asked for his input. The gig was just for me. As we were business partners, I felt it needed to be discussed.

He took a surprisingly hard line on my accepting this offer. "If you take this job, I won't be here for you when you return."

Wow, talk about forcing an issue. I was usually on the other side of these discussions. Now I was getting a taste of what it was like dealing with Kevin—and by default, me. As I tried to reason with him, he felt the strike could be settled at any time. If it was, he needed to go out and find some work. He couldn't or wouldn't wait for me to return, which made sense. Deeply rooted inside of me, I almost felt this was the opportunity I was waiting for. What was meant to be would be.

Boy, that sentiment couldn't have been truer. Two weeks into the trip, my wife tracked me down in Bangkok to tell me the strike was over.

I called Kevin to get some details. He told me that the news was true, and he was putting out feelers for work on his own.

I had no choice. I couldn't abandon the folks I was chaperoning. So I wished him luck. He asked if I had any problems with his talking to our agent, Herb Karp; asking him to represent Kevin as an individual. What could I say other than, "*gay ga zinta hate*." That's Yiddish for "go in good health."

For the rest of the trip, I wondered what would greet me when I got back to Los Angeles. Everyone knew me as part of the boys, Hartigan and Garber. We were thought of as one. How was I going to restart my career as a solo act?

ONE LAST SHOT

I returned and immediately began trying to drum up some work. I sent out letters and made phone calls. Quickly I learned how despised we had become. Many people refused to take my call. If they did, they'd ask, "Garber, which one are you—the funny one or the one who can write?" Strange question, yes? I knew I was going to have to create a new identity for myself, and fast, if I was going to rebound.

I called around to a few agencies to see if they were interested in handling me. No one even nibbled. I called Herb Karp, my old William Morris agent, and the only one in town, it seemed, who'd talk to me. Not only was interested, he said, but he was leaving William Morris to start his own agency. He'd like me to be one of his first clients. He also told me he was not going to be taking on Kevin. He felt my former partner was too toxic for a new agency.

Surprising myself, I told Herb he could do worse. I told him that Kevin had so much talent—and the two of them had been through so much over the years—that he should reconsider and take Kevin on as well—; just separately from me. Herb, though, was adamant and cautioned me, "the farther you stay from him, the better off you're going to be."

My chance to prove myself as an individual came a few days later. While I was busy writing up a spec pilot, an episode Herb could take around to show off my solo talents, he phoned and said he had an interview for me. It was at Bob Banner & Associates, and of all places to be located, they were at the Pacific Design Center in West Hollywood. People living in Los Angeles call that building the Big Blue Whale for its neo-modern architecture with an exterior of cobalt blue reflective glass, which stands tall on Melrose Avenue. It was a close drive for me coming from the Hills. My wife and I loved going to that building as it housed shops specializing in the most fashion-forward design of furniture and artistic pieces. It is as far away from a traditional studio as you could get.

"*Weekdays*," Bob Banner revealed, "Is the name of the new talk/service show that we're piloting." It was going to be a strip show—meaning it aired five days a week. They were going to combine talk, interviews, comedy, music, cooking, fashion and all of the other successful elements that were making this kind of daytime fair so popular. Soap operas were fading. Game shows were dying. Variety was dead. What was flourishing were shows hosted by the likes of Mike Douglas, Merv Griffin, Dinah Shore and Oprah Winfrey. These personalities were carrying shows that made the housewife viewer feel very comfortable in their style of life.

Bob, the owner of the company and a longtime industry professional, was going to executive produce. Along with him was co-producer and director, Don Weiner. They had just chosen their hostess for the show—a young actress/singer, named Kathy Lee Johnson. She was featured on *Name That Tune* (known as the La-la Lady), she had been on *Hee-Haw Honey*, the country and western themed variety spin-off from *Hee-Haw* and she had recently been doing some remote human interest stories for *Good Morning, America*.

I found out in the next few weeks that she was a joy to work with. She loved to laugh and had that magnetic characteristic—affability. You could see why she had been chosen to take the on-camera reins of this new series. This would be a great break for her. A few years later, she would become better known to the world after her marriage to husband, Frank. She now goes by her married name, Kathy Lee Gifford. To most, she's simply known as, Kathy Lee.

"We need a head writer. Do you think you can do that?" Bob Banner asked me. He and Don Weiner seemed to be genuinely interested in me. They liked my personality, my answers to their questions and most of all, my enthusiasm.

"You mean, alone? No. But with a small staff, sure." That was the truthful answer. They confided that they had two other people they were considering for staff, but they needed someone with my background—a show runner, writer and producer whose resume covered the entertainment gamut—sitcoms, pilots, variety shows, even game shows. When you summed it all up, on paper, I was their guy.

What they failed to take into consideration is that all of my success was shared. Kevin was at my side. This was my first interview alone in ten years. I had been a solo act for all of about 48 hours. And here they were offering me the job of producer/head writer. C'mon, it's Hollywood. Of course I said, "Yes."

There was one codicil that I added. I would get to choose the staff. Both Bob and Don agreed. They gave me the names of the two guys they were interested in, but said I could choose them or anyone else.

So I met the two guys. They were very nice. They had some daytime experience, but like me, most of their background was in sitcoms. I really felt that to complement my lack of experience in talk shows, I could use a seasoned pro. I really only knew one. I knew he was out of work and most likely available.

I called Kevin who was reluctant at first. In his mind it stung that I, the untalented member of the team (at least in Kevin's eyes compared to him), would not only have found work so fast, but as a producer/head writer. I asked my former partner if he thought he could work with me and another guy under my leadership. He would be reporting to me and not be my equal. And if it was too uncomfortable, he could just pass. Kevin came in to meet with me as well as Bob and Don. As they ran the show, I thought it would be best for them to meet Kevin before I officially hired him.

Kevin came in before noon and met the guys. They liked him. He was his typical funny, humorous self. They appreciated that he had experience having worked on the daytime talker starring Dinah Shore. Neither he nor I shared the ignominious firing Kevin got from that star and that show. It was best not spoken of at this juncture. So, in a matter of minutes, Kevin was my first hire.

As Kevin and I settled into our chairs to get to work, executive producer Bob stuck his head into the office to make sure everything was okay. Kevin then started cracking jokes and ridiculing some of the performers Bob had worked for in the past; Carol Burnett, Dinah Shore, John Davidson and Garry Moore. Banner was a very dignified businessman, soft-spoken and polite to a flaw. He'd never seen nor heard a malcontent like Kevin before—and he wasn't going to hear from him again either. Bob called me out of the office and told me to have Kevin removed from the show. He couldn't work with such a destructive, mean-spirited, insulting personality. His company prided itself on kinship and family values. Kevin demonstrated he lacked those both.

Now was my moment of truth. I flashed to our breakup when Kevin called the shots and separated from me during the strike. It stung at that time, but it was something I had anticipated and it wasn't something I had to do. At that point, I felt it more of a relief, freedom from his shackles. It was what I wanted... And deep down inside, I was prepared for it.

But now I was the one on the hot seat. I was going to have to take action. I would have to remove Kevin from a situation that existed, not a vague continuation of something that no longer really endured. This was real. I was going to be stepping into Kevin shoes—controlling a situation. Bob Banner had put me in the position of the tiny bird being forced out of the nest for the first time, either to fly or perish.

I took a breath. Instead of being pushed, I jumped, preferring to control my own destiny. Down I fell, flapping and praying. Then a miracle happened. I didn't go splat on the ground below. My wings took me into flight. Higher and higher I flew. Not wobbly, uncertainly aerodynamics; I truly soared.

I took Kevin aside, confidently told him the unsparing truth which I think he actually knew was coming. There was a momentary silence—this is where Kevin normally would have kicked into another gear—the offensive barrage. Instead of the Guernica, he took a totally new tack. Submission. Once I told him in so many words that he was through, and "we" were truly done for good, he looked at me and said, "Boychick, you make me proud. I taught you well, grasshopper. You not only grew a pair of balls, you learned how to use them. Now go out and knock 'em dead."

And with that he walked out of the office, out of the building and soon after, out of the industry. But one place he never walked out of was my heart.

This became the professional end for Hartigan and Garber. It could have ended when we left Viacom, but I wasn't strong enough or confident enough to go it on my own, until this point. Maybe it was Bob Banner who made me the individual that I became professionally. Maybe it was the discovery of something inside of me—a confidence I actually had. Regardless, I'd never have found it without the master showman.

Though a personal friendship continues to this day, Kevin and I never would again sit down to write together. We'd talk, we'd dine and we'd swap stories.

Kevin's career screeched to a halt. He never did recapture the magic he once had. I, on the other hand, would flourish and spend the next 20 years writing and producing television shows, even picking up a few awards along the way. My career continues today. As a matter of fact, I have a script due in three...

The cellphone rang. I snapped out of my reminiscences and looked over to the source of the ringing. In the caller ID window I could see it was coming from the 781 area code—Boston. And the number wasn't Helen's but rather Kevin's. I recognized it. Was this the call that would tell me something I prayed to hear? Or the call I was dreading? The phone's familiar ring tone continued, ironically the one I had picked for this device—*Feelin' Alright*.

It continued as I stared at the cellphone in my hand.

All I had to do was press the "receive" button. While I stared at it, hesitating, it suddenly went silent. I don't know exactly why I didn't take this call. It was like not wanting to know the final score of a close Red Sox game. As long as I didn't hear it, there was still hope.

PING. I heard another familiar signal tone. An icon now appeared on my cell. The caller had left a message.

I needed a few more minutes before I'd have the strength to retrieve the words. Was Kevin miraculously still with us? Is Kevin a contemporary Lazarus rising, or had he gone to legend, destined to dine at the Friars Club dais in the sky with Frank Sinatra, Jack Benny and Groucho Marx? All of them were his heroes.

I finished my spring cleaning. I threw away almost nothing; filled up on career reflections. It was time now to check my voice mail. I pressed the number "1" to hear my message. It was Helen who simply said, "call back."

I did. And the phone answered on the second ring.

"Hey, this is Kevin. If you're hearing this message, it's because I'm dead."

This was followed by a musical verse sung by the Manhattan Transfer, asking the operator to ring up Jesus in heaven. Leave it to Kevin to announce his own passing with a pre-arranged, orchestrated message. A showman to the end.

Now, my good friend, my mentor and my partner was gone. All that is left to do is bid him "Farewell." I just hope he doesn't turn Heaven into the hell he turned Hollywood into.

My decision not to take his liver was arrived at for a number of reasons, but this is not about me. This story is about Kevin Hartigan, a one of a kind, larger-than-life character. Maybe we're all a little better for Kevin touching our lives. I know I am.

Shalom my sweet Shabbat Goy.

THE END

JUST A BIT MORE

In case you want to find out more about Kevin, his antics and enjoy some of the master's tips on self-promoting yourself from obscurity to fame and then to oblivion, visit us at www.HollywoodHuckster.wordpress.com

ACKNOWLEDGEMENTS

Bill Braunstein

Larry Levy

Joe Hahle

Tom Szollosi

Ida Garber

Christopher Ming

Daniel Reyes

Kalman Kaminer

Richard Goldman

Eric Epstein

30049849R00166

Made in the USA
Charleston, SC
02 June 2014